T0208369

Never Miss a Beat

An Evocation of the Heart

Jessie K. Stern

iUniverse, Inc.
New York Bloomington

Never Miss a Beat

An Evocation Of The Heart

iUniverse books may be ordered through booksellers or by contacting:

iUniverse
1663 Liberty Drive
Bloomington, IN 47403
www.iuniverse.com
1-800-Authors (1-800-288-4677)

ISBN: 978-1-4401-7967-9 (pbk)
ISBN: 978-1-4401-7968-6 (ebk)

Printed in the United States of America
iUniverse rev. date: 7/15/10

"Go Forth"

Lech L'chah

"To A Place That I Will Show You"

El Haaretz Asher Areka

The King said,
“That moment I shall never forget.”
“You will, though,
Unless you make a memorandum of it.”
Lewis Carroll

With love for

SHELLY

EMILY, NOAH, GAYLE AND GARY

JOSH, ARI, EBAN, SETH, JEREMY AND HILDY

IRVING AND FAMILY

Contents

PREFACE

As far back as I can remember, I can't recall not having thought about the mystery of life -- sometimes in ecstatic wonderment, sometimes in fear and trembling. Perhaps it is in my genes. Perhaps I brought it with me from a previous life. Perhaps it is part of being human. In short, *the* ineluctability of life will be explored in this memoir, as well as the tale of my heart.

According to a social science class at the University of Michigan/Dearborn in 2001, most human beings have an urge to leave a legacy. The older we get, the stronger the urge becomes. My professor called this phenomenon "gerontivity," a word, I believe, he originated. I confess that I suffer from this malady. Hence, I bow to gerontivity by leaving this memoir for my family and friends as well as for any reader who acknowledges the struggles and challenges of being human.

My primary motivation for sharing this lifetime of personal stories is the act of writing, which unleashes within me a yearning for creativity. When satisfied, this urge has the additional benefit of releasing the power of healing. I apologize for using the reader to assuage my neediness.

While it is not the purpose of this memoir to lecture, given the fullness of my experience, a bit of advice might unwittingly slip into the text from time to time. After all, age is reputed to enhance wisdom. You be the judge!

I extend my gratitude and profound respect to those who have the fortitude to join me on this journey.

INTRODUCTION

It seems fitting that this life review begin with my legacy. Its brevity will not do justice to the indebtedness I owe my parents and grandparents and other members of my family. We are all heirs of those who came before us.

Information about my mother's family is sketchy. I would like to know more, but everyone who could have filled in the blanks with their stories and memories has either died or forgotten the details. I do know the family emigrated from Eastern Europe and settled in Chicago. From genealogical research, I learned that both of my maternal grandparents came from Russia and Lithuania, probably Maripol.

My grandmother's name was Jessie. I believe she died while my mother was pregnant with me. When my mother spoke of her, it was always with a degree of sadness. Her death was obviously a huge and unbearable loss for my mother. I was told that my grandma was a tall woman, which was unusual for our family. Her eyes were blue. I have seen pictures of her. I liked her face, and her posture was erect. In photos, she appeared to be a strong woman, yet I found in her bearing a reflection of a gentle nature. I am sorry I did not know her. I wish she had left an autobiography. I am proud to carry her name.

My mother told me that, although her father, Philip, was a very observant Jew, he never foisted his religiosity on his children. He owned a small furniture store in Chicago. In those days, Saturday was the busiest retail day of the week. Stores were closed only on Sundays and holidays and generally not opened any evenings. Yet, in spite of the financial sacrifice, Grandpa Philip closed his store on Saturdays in observance of the Sabbath. I loved the portrait we had of him in our home, and I remember his handsome face. Unfortunately, it disappeared after my mother died.

My Aunt Eileen, a daughter-in-law, told me she loved my grandparents. They were very good to her. Grandma and Grandpa had 12 children, but only five survived to adulthood. My mother's only living siblings were my Aunt Bella, who died in her 40's when I was about nine years old; Uncle Arthur, the oldest of the living children, who was a dentist as was his younger brother, Bernard (who we called Uncle Bobby and was married to Aunt Eileen); and Aunt Ada, who was married to Uncle George. My mother, Gertrude, was the youngest.

It was Uncle Arthur who changed the family name from Finkelstein to Field sometime in the 1920s when he married Aunt Frieda who wanted a more American sounding name. They had two children, Victor and Margie. Victor was about ten years older than I. He adored my mother and was good to me. He never married and died some years ago. Margie was never as warm to me as her brother was, and I lost touch with her years ago. I believe she died about ten years ago from breast cancer.

Uncle Bobby and Aunt Eileen had two children, Joanne and Philip who live in Las Vegas. Joyfully, I am in touch with both of them. Aunt Bella and her husband, Uncle Max adopted two girls, Marion and Henrietta. Henrietta, whom we called Yetta, was about my age. We played together as children, but I am sorry that I have lost touch with both of them. In fact I have lost track of all of my mother's family except for my cousin Joanne. Aunt Ada and Uncle George had no children.

I recall my mother telling me about my great-grandfather, Lazarus Finkelstein, who died in Chicago at 109 years old in 1918. *The Chicago Examiner* included an interview with Lazarus on his 107th birthday, as well as his obituary. He was truly a remarkable man. During tours at Waldheim Cemetery, Chicago's largest Jewish cemetery, Lazarus' grave is included. The supervisor of the cemetery told me, "There is a photograph of him on his grave stone which I love. He is beautiful."

Jessie's great-grandfather, Lazarus Finkelstein, and his wife

My father's family came from Odessa, Russia. He told me that Kaufman was not the original family name. For years I thought their name was Kretchmer. When my husband and I were in Israel many years later, we visited the Museum of the Diaspora genealogy department. When I looked up Kretchmer from Odessa, my effort drew a blank. Then in 1997, my father's first cousin, Harry Karchmer, who was completing a genealogy of the entire "Karchmer" family, discovered my brother and me. It then became apparent to me that I had misunderstood my dad when he told me the family name.

To this day no one knows how our part of the family got the name Kaufman, but Harry provided every member of the Karchmer/Kaufman dynasty with a complete genealogy going back six generations. Harry Karchmer and his wonderful wife Paula have become a treasure to me. We first met in 1998 when they came all the way from Tucson, Arizona to our granddaughter Emily Eubank's Bat Mitzvah in 1998. It was love at first sight! At that moment I felt we had known each other forever

My paternal grandfather, Nathan Kaufman, was drafted in the Russo-Japanese War. He suffered abuse because of the rampant anti-Semitism in the Russian army. In what some would call an act of betrayal, but I call an act of bravery, Grandpa deserted the army and brought his family to America in 1904. Perhaps, he changed his last name motivated by the fear that the Russian army might find him in the USA and bring him back to Russia to be shot. I regret that I never got the details of his escape. I feel so grateful to him for taking that heroic and dangerous step as a young man. Thousands of Jewish families escaped the pogroms and hate of Eastern Europe at the end of the 19th and early 20th centuries, which saved them from annihilation in the Holocaust fifty year's later. Thanks to Grandpa, and others like him, my generation is here to tell the tale.

Grandpa was married to Leah Levin. She had a brother who lived in Indiana Harbor, Indiana, which is probably why the family moved there. Grandma was a jovial and loving woman whom I adored.

I am eternally grateful to relatives on both sides of my family. My story follows theirs.

March 1997

Leah and Nathan Kaufman, early 20th century

ACKNOWLEDGMENTS

This book would not have been possible without the support and encouragement of many friends and writers. I set this project aside countless times over the past nine years. Writer's block, other pressing responsibilities, doubt about my ability to deal with the material, and the disturbing question of whether my writing skills were up to the challenge were concerns which, at times, made it difficult to continue.

Fortunately, I did not keep the project a secret. Speaking about it was my way of reaching out. Many gave me encouragement to continue, but my friend, Doris Spivack, went one step further by offering her help. She made suggestions about publishing, addressing the issue of the cover design and, finally, even agreed to read much of the text. I gratefully took advantage of many of her suggestions. Thank you, Doris. You cannot take blame for the finished product but much credit for whatever is best in my work is gratefully offered here.

In May, 2005, I received an unexpected invitation to attend the Bear River Writers' Conference, sponsored by the University of Michigan. I never thought of myself as a writer, so I wondered how I got on the mailing list, a mystery which, in spite of much probing, remains unsolved. The conference is held at Camp Michigania on Walloon Lake, just a few miles southwest of Petoskey, an important resort area in northern Michigan. The timing of the conference was perfect. When the invitation arrived, my memoir and its writer needed a boost. I was hesitant to attend, not sure I was qualified, but an angel sitting on my shoulder kept whispering, "Try it. Certainly, you will be nervous and undoubtedly humbled, but the crowd will not be boring, and you might even learn something!" I listened to my angel, mindful that receiving the invitation may not have been a coincidence. Indeed, it may have been mailed by the angel, herself.

Bear River proved to be everything the angel suggested it would be. For three consecutive years, I packed my laptop, a few camp outfits, my memoir and a bathing suit and headed north, in early June. I pay humble tribute to my workshop leaders; Richard McCann in 2005; Laura Kasischke in 2006; and Bob Hicok in 2007. They are distinguished professors and published authors, as well as stellar teachers. Their writing assignments in class, homework each evening and personal critiques were reassuring, as well as constructive and provided profound insight into my work.

Chris Lord is another Bear River treasure. I first learned what a gifted poet she is when we shared Laura Kashschke's workshop. I was immediately drawn to her gentle manner, which belied her many accomplishments. Besides being the organizer of this incredible writers' conference, Chris is the founder and editor of the annual Bear River Review, an on line journal of selected writings of Bear River students and instructors. After two successful years in the online format, Chris decided to add a print edition, *Bear River Writers Respond to War*. Thanks to Chris, I have the good fortune of being published in the three online versions of the "Bear River Review," as well as in the 2007 print version.

And finally I want to thank Professor Keith Taylor who took time from his demanding schedule as director of the conference to have lunch with me. I will forever be grateful for his several publishing suggestions to this novice writer. Lunch with him in June 2007 was a Bear River highlight.

I was also blessed with incredible classmates. We spent 10 hours together over the four days of the conference, sharing our lives with one another, reading our material to one another, making gentle but on target comments and suggestions to one another and, most importantly, encouraging each other. The experience refreshed my commitment to complete this project and gave me the confidence to read my poetry, which, prior to Bear River, had remained in the closet, and had never been shared. It was also exciting to come home with rough drafts of a number of new pieces. It feels good to shout an effervescent accolade for Bear River from the roof tops!

Less than a year ago I had the good fortune to join the Writers' Corner at the Jewish Community Center in Oak Park. Under the tutelage of Professor Norma Goldman, who founded the group 50 years ago, Writers' Corner has provided a venue for aspiring and accomplished writers to read their work and learn from the comments of their peers. I am honored to be part of this distinguished group of writers and thank Norma for inviting me to become a member.

My indebtedness to all of those I have honored has the additional components of appreciation and affection.

IN THE BEGINNING
Beresheet

Gratefully, the world accepted the first beat of my heart on May 8, 1931, when Effie Lobdel, my mother's obstetrician, brought me into the world -- kicking and screaming -- at Michael Reese Hospital, in Chicago.

I was named after my maternal grandmother. My parents, Gertrude and Harry Kaufman, gave me the middle name Joy, which supports my belief that despite the difficult times in which I was born, they were happy to have me.

Harry and Gertrude Kaufman, circa 1927

In those days, women physicians were rare. It was out of the ordinary to go to a "lady doctor." I don't think my mom realized that selecting Effie made her an early feminist. She proved then, as she did for the rest of her short life, that she was no ordinary woman. The times were not ordinary, either. In the midst of the Great Depression, money had no value. There were no jobs, banks were defaulting, and people were poor, hungry and desperate. Though we did not have much money, we always had food on our table and were never cold. But it was never easy. The Kaufman family was seriously affected by the Great Depression. Although they did not lose the family business, Kaufman's Hardware, they lost the building that housed the store. It was a stately brick building with a large flat upstairs where we eventually lived. Years later, I remember what a celebratory day it was for the family to buy the building back.

My earliest memories go back to an apartment with two small bedrooms and a bathroom in East Chicago, Indiana. My mother had invited her aunt, who was widowed young and childless, to live with us. Aunt Rae slept on a Murphy bed in the living room. She was my Grandma Jessie's sister, a generation older than my mother. She sold corsets at the Boston Store, a medium-priced department store in Chicago. Thanks to women's liberation, most women today do not know what a corset is. They were tight, constricting and very uncomfortable.

To make matters worse for Aunt Rae, she had to take a 45-minute ride on the South Shore train to work six days a week. Five-day-a-week jobs were unheard of back then. It was a difficult job, standing on her feet for long hours. Her ankles were always swollen, but I never heard her complain. She was a gentle, loving woman, and I adored her. She took my side whenever there was an issue between my mother and me. She would say, "Gertie, she didn't mean it." Aunt Rae was my best friend.

Aunt Rae and Jessie, 1936

I started kindergarten at the Harrison School in East Chicago and was adjusting nicely, until one day matters deteriorated. My mother had come to school with me. I started working on a project with some of my classmates, and forgot she was there. The kids were doing something dumb that needed fixing; so, in no uncertain terms, I told them I had a better way to fix it. My teacher, Miss Cobb witnessed the incident. Later, I overheard her tell my mother, "Jessie, has a tendency to be dictatorial." On the way home, I said, "Mommy, what does dictatorial mean?" There was a pause. "It means bossy," she said. "Try not to be bossy anymore." I could tell she was upset. "I will, Mommy," I said.

My approach in school softened, becoming less forceful, less strident, and less "bossy." Miss Cobb and my mother never called me dictatorial again. The kids at school actually started to like me. I did not realize it then, but I was becoming a leader. Over time, I learned to listen to other points of view and started to approach my goals through consensus, which not only improved my interpersonal relations, but also improved the chance for a positive outcome. I continued to receive leadership roles in high school, college and in my adult life, which, for the most part, has become a source of pleasure and accomplishment, in spite of the continuing visage of the original guilt.

Our move to Indiana Harbor when I was 10 years old was prompted by the heart attack Grandpa had while he and Grandma were still living in the flat over the hardware store with my father's brother, whom we called Uncle Duke. They were partners at the hardware store with Grandpa. The doctor advised him to retire and move to Los Angeles where his daughter, Frieda, lived with her husband, Uncle Leo. When Grandma and Grandpa left for California, we moved into the flat with Aunt Rae and joined Uncle Duke, who remained in Indiana Harbor. We were now a family of five.

I missed the grass and trees that surrounded our former apartment in East Chicago, but my father did not have to take the bus to work anymore, and our home was a spacious three- bedroom apartment with a living room, library, kitchen, large dining room and one bathroom with a sink and an old fashioned bathtub on legs. Eventually, my father added an improvised shower in the tub.

Our kitchen was large and square with a doorway into a pantry. It had an old fashioned ice-box. Food was kept cold by large blocks of ice replaced by regular visits from the ice-man. A large, square wooden prep table sat in the middle of the room. A small table placed next to the enormous gas stove on legs was the location of a weekly family ritual. Every Sunday night after dinner, we would gather around our wooden radio, which became the center of the universe, and listen to Jack Benny, Burns and Allen, and Eddie Cantor. Roaring with laughter as a family was our favorite time of the week.

I loved to watch Grandma make challah, chopped liver, chopped herring and gefilte fish. I can still see her walking around the kitchen, cradling a huge wooden bowl in her left arm, talking and chopping at the same time. Everything was chopped by hand. On Fridays, when Grandma made challah, she always gave me special miniature braided challah of my very own. I adored her.

The windows over the sink at the back of the kitchen overlooked a screened porch and a staircase that led to the garage where my father stored his truck. I loved that truck. There were no seat belts in those days and no laws about buckling up, so once in a while I got to ride in the back of the truck. That is probably where my love of convertibles began.

We had a coal-burning furnace with steam radiators. The furnace was in the basement, and my father had to go down there early on winter mornings to stoke the furnace and add coal before his bath. It was a dirty job. One of my favorite memories was watching Daddy's routine dressing and preparing himself for work. I can still see him in front of his bureau, looking in the mirror, combing his hair, then in the same order, putting his watch on, his wallet in his back pocket, and placing a handkerchief in the breast pocket of his jacket. He always wore a clean shirt and tie, and a vest in the winter. I was enchanted. He was an adorable man, fun-loving, with a winning personality. Everybody in town loved Harry Kaufman. He was the magnet that attracted customers to our store.

Indiana Harbor was a small steel town in Indiana, 20 miles southeast from Chicago on Lake Michigan. The Inland Steel Company was the town's anchor, located a few blocks from the store at the water's edge. Huge steam ships arrived daily from Minnesota unloading cargoes of iron ore and limestone. The view from our living room window was a sky covered with black smoke. My mother complained about cleaning the ever-present black soot on the window sills and furniture of our flat.

In school, most of the kids were poorer. Inland Steel, where jobs were plentiful, drew a huge immigrant population of Mexicans, Poles, and African-Americans, whom we called Negroes. I had no trouble making friends with any of the school population, although my closest friends were other Jewish girls.

In fifth grade, our class toured the Inland Steel factory. Huge fires producing an eerie light were everywhere, yet darkness permeated the work area. It was boiling hot, and perspiring men in their undershirts worked the blast furnaces. It upset me to see them working so hard. The heat, the darkness, the loud machines and the eerie light frightened me. I could not wait to get back to school.

In contrast, Kaufman's Hardware Store at 3526 Main St. was beautiful. I know it is hard to imagine that a hardware store can be beautiful, but this one was. Picture an outdoor entrance of small green and white tiles with the word "Kaufman" embedded in the ground. Two large display windows framed the outdoor lobby, and two entrances into the store were found on either side of a small center display window. The ample space inside was covered with lovely oak floors. The center of the store was filled with display tables. The walls were lined with sturdy oak cabinets, where tools and other items were arranged on red felt. Counters and drawers stored more merchandise. Towards the rear of the store, a wide stairway led to an open balcony, which served as an office, where my mother worked part time as a secretary. I loved running up and down those stairs. More storage was found under the balcony, and an attached garage housed the delivery truck.

My father took special pride in decorating the store's display windows. He changed them frequently, generally on Sundays when all the stores were closed. For me, there was nothing more enjoyable on a Sunday than to watch him trim the windows. His finished windows reflected the calendar, and were an inviting presentation of the seasons and holidays. His Christmas windows were especially prize-worthy. People always stopped to admire them. Kaufman's was a hardware store with a touch of class.

After school and Sundays, I hung around the store as much as I could. I loved being with my father. One day he said to me, "Jess, will you unpack and sort a few cartons of stock that just came in?" I was excited by the assignment. When I finished a few hours later, I saw my father approaching. Bet he's coming over to check out my handiwork, I thought. As he examined what I had done, I noticed he was not smiling. "Jess, this isn't right," he said. "I'll have George do it." Though, he was not angry, my heart sank. Shame engulfed me as I held back tears. In that moment I learned what it felt like to be a failure.

Grandma and Grandpa moved to an apartment in Venice, California, a suburban beach community near Los Angeles. My parents and I went to California to visit them and took *El Capitan,* a streamlined high-speed train. It took two days and three nights to reach Los Angeles from Chicago, and we traveled coach. We could not afford the Pullman car, which had bunk beds, so we had to sit up all night.

One night, a big handsome man took a pillow and sprawled out in the aisle. Everyone talked about it the next morning. Little did anyone know that he was Victor Mature, a future Hollywood star. I was enthralled by his size and good looks. It was exciting to see him in the movies. I bet he never traveled coach again! It was also the first time I ever saw real mountains and a real desert. When I wasn't looking at Victor Mature, I had my nose glued to the train window. I got to eat in the dining car and play cards in the club car. What thrills for an eight-year-old girl.

California was a wonderland. Main Street in Indiana was bereft of trees, but in Los Angeles there were palm trees everywhere. I couldn't believe the prevalence of the flowers, and the grass was so green. Indiana Harbor had Lake Michigan; Los Angeles had the Pacific Ocean. The first time I saw the Pacific from the beach, I was awe-struck. I remember trembling. Mind you, it did not look any different than Lake Michigan, except the waves were more fierce and the air was cleaner; but viewing the largest body of water on Earth was like contemplating the vastness of the Universe. When I finally got the nerve to put a toe in the water and began to play, the fear and awe evaporated. Instead, I was shocked by the salt water, which tasted terrible and burned my eyes. To this day, I still prefer to swim and play in the fresh water of Lake Michigan.

California not only looked different but smelled different. Now, 68 years later, I can still conjure up the "California smells," and recall with delight the sweet sensation of being warm in the winter and seeing things like pink sidewalks and pink houses and swimming pools everywhere. I went to L.A. again when I was about 12 years old with only my father. It was nice having him all to myself. Mother stayed home, and I'm not sure if it was because of the expense, or because my brother was only two years old and they thought he was too young to take such a long trip. The wonderful smells and green grass were still there, and so was the sunshine. Nothing had changed.

Life in Indiana Harbor had not changed either. The Vic Movie Theatre was still across the street from our store. I went to the movies nearly every Saturday afternoon, and loved cowboy movies and cartoons, especially Popeye. My father loved it, too. Everything was in black and white. For 15 cents we saw a double feature, cartoons and a weekly recap of the week's war news called, "The March of Time". It always scared me, and I've hated wars ever since.

My friends at Lincoln School in Indiana Harbor were both boys and girls. After school we played in the alley behind the store. We bounced balls off the buildings and played lots of catch. My dad taught me how to catch. He also took me to baseball games. We went to see the Chicago White Sox and the Chicago Cubs. I loved the Cubs and Wrigley Field, the only ballpark with ivy covering the outfield wall. It remains one of the few old stadiums still in use. I still love playing catch, even with a baseball glove, and I throw properly by turning to the side and using my shoulder, like guys do.

My friends and I often played on the asphalt roof of our store, which was an extension of our flat and covered the garage and the back of the store. The roof was my "backyard". The buildings on either side of our building were very close. One day, I was playing "cops and robbers" on the roof with a few of the boys from school. There was a chase scene, and the only way to escape was for the good guys to make a four-foot jump to the next building. If we jumped and missed, we would fall two stories to the concrete walkway below. I was terrified, but I didn't want the guys to call me a sissy, so I jumped! After the game was over and I had jumped back, I was shaking with fear, but was I ever proud of myself.

I can't remember who won the chase, but I'll never forget what happened next. My parents confronted me when they heard about my escapade. I denied the charges, but when the truth came out, I was punished as much for lying as for my daringly foolish behavior. I became a hero to my partners-in-crime, but it was a big price to pay. Guilt taught me two lessons: when you do something "naughty," you get caught, and lying doesn't pay in the end. That was the last time I ever tried the jump. As for lying, well, I decided to try to be good!

Hot Sundays in the summertime often centered on going to the beach, about 20 minutes from Indiana

Harbor. The beach was like heaven. I loved to wiggle my toes in the sand, float on an inner-tube and play catch with the other kids. We usually met friends or cousins there. Everyone brought wonderful homemade food and we picnicked in the park behind the beach. No one liked sand in their food!

Back then it was not common for ordinary people to participate in sports, especially women. Golf was considered a game for the rich, yet my mother knew how to play golf, swim and ride a bike. Most of her female friends did not engage in athletics. It was important to her that I have these skills.

When I was five she taught me how to ride a bike. There were no training wheels in those days. I remember she held the bike up by grasping the back of the seat and running with the moving bike as I pedaled. It took me many tries and many days to relax and get it right. I was a "scaredy cat" in those days. My mother was my hero. She had battle scars from the pedals hitting her shins as she clutched the wobbling bike by the seat. She also bought me a small set of golf clubs when I was about twelve and started to occasionally take me out to play nine holes at Mac Arthur Park, a par 3 course. Neither of us was proficient, but I learned the etiquette of golf. And we had fun. So began my life long love hate relationship with the game of golf which I still consider one of life's greatest challenges.

Jessie, 1936

A milestone event in my life was the birth of my baby brother, Irving Hanan, January 10, 1941, when I was 10 years old. His middle name was selected in memory of our Aunt Bella, whose first name was Hannah, my mother's sister who had died shortly before Irv was born. I am not sure about the origin of his first name. I think he was named for someone in our dad's family named Isaac. Our parents had waited a long time for him. I remember often overhearing my mother saying to her friends, "Irving's arrival is the happiest moment in my life since Jessie Joy was born."

Harry, Gertrude, Jessie, and baby Irving Kaufman, 1941

The Kaufmans, circa 1942

He was a cute little guy with a winning personality, and of course, he was very smart. I enjoyed him, but I did not like baby sitting on Saturday afternoons when I preferred being with my friends. My mom and I agreed on a compromise. I could meet my friends at the movies, but Irv had to go with me. Irv suggests that I left him alone while I *kibbitzed* with my girlfriends for extensive periods of time. The length of my bathroom excursions is in dispute and may never be resolved. But I still loved you, Irv. Having a baby brother, in spite of Saturday afternoons, definitely enriched my life.

I pretty much did the things little girls do when they are growing up. I periodically switched best friends, did sleepovers and kept a diary with the primary subject being, "boys." When our parents let us, we loved to talk to each other on the telephone. There were no cell phones back then. I loved meeting my girlfriends for lunch in Chicago on Saturdays, shopping at Marshall Field's or going to the Chicago Theater for a movie and a stage show before taking the South Shore back to East Chicago.

The live stage shows at the Chicago Theater were amazing and featured a famous entertainer, all for the price of a ticket to the movies. I enjoyed my friends, and had my share of boyfriends. My favorite boyfriend at the time was Phil Pecar, a second cousin. Philly used to take me to AZA dances. AZA was a teen age group for Jewish boys, sponsored by B'nai B'rith. One year I was voted AZA Sweetheart. I dated Phil occasionally when we were both at Indiana University. He eventually married one of my sorority pledge sisters and settled in Indianapolis. Sadly, both died recently.

Sometime before the arrival of my baby brother, Aunt Rae gave me a Victrola record player, which I loved. Picture a box with a large megaphone device protruding from the top. Before electrical record players were available, the Victrola had to be wound by hand with a crank on the side of the box to play 78 r.p.m. records. My first exposure to classical music was a recording of the Tchaikovsky Piano Concerto. I played it over and over, enjoying it more each time I heard it. Mom also took me to concerts in East Chicago whenever a traveling orchestra or soloist was in town.

The music revealed a world which became a lifetime love, but it wasn't always that way. After a pathetic effort to study violin from age six to 10 with encouragement and patience from my teacher, Joe Cohen, I had not advanced beyond first position. It was time to give up. Mr. Cohen and my parents were relieved. They no longer had to listen to me practice any more.

But my musical fortunes changed in fifth grade with a required class in Music Appreciation and my teacher, Mr. Fox. Extremely thin, red hair and a huge adam's apple, the kids made fun of him, but I thought he was awesome. He taught us about the four movements in a classical symphony and how each was structured. We studied Beethoven's Fifth Symphony; the music was gorgeous.

By the time I turned 12, all my friends were taking piano lessons and I felt left out. I really wanted to try it, but we did not have a piano. Though it would be a financial challenge, my mother's attitude was, "Nothing is too good for my Jessie Joy." When I came home from school on my birthday, I found a six-foot ebony Mason and Hamlin Grand piano in our living room. I was ecstatic.

My piano teacher was Sarah, a no-nonsense teacher whose love of music was infectious. And she was expensive -- five dollars for a one-hour lesson. Every Saturday morning I took a 30-minute ride on the South Shore train to downtown Chicago, transferred to the Washington Street bus for another 30-minute ride to Sarah's house. Though she was demanding, Sarah engendered in me respect and love for her. I could not afford to disappoint her, so I practiced. More than anything she was an inspiration.

Four years after I began taking piano lessons, they were abruptly discontinued when my father died. But the dye was cast. I have adored the sound of a piano ever since. I recently started playing again: nothing difficult, but sitting at the piano for an hour brings me great joy. And my original piano has always been in good hands. After Mother died, Uncle Arthur, a pianist, kept the instrument in his apartment for many years. Jeremy and his family have it have it now. Shelly and I have a smaller Mason and Hamlin baby grand in the living room of our Franklin home. The piano, which we acquired from Phyllis Loewenstein, had been a gift from her father when she was a child.

Being 12 years old was a marker year for me. As with the piano, my parents made a gallant effort to find the money to fulfill yet another of my extravagant dreams. I wanted to go to summer camp with my girlfriends. I was overwhelmed when I saw Camp Mac-Do Lodge in Delavan, Wisconsin for the first time. Greeting me was a white wooden mansion sitting majestically on a hill, surrounded by grass as green as it was in California. The mansion, which served as dining room, recreation room and administrative office, stood apart from the neatly arranged cabins where the campers lived, and the lawn meandered down to the edge of a sparkling blue lake.

The happiest summers of my childhood were spent in at Mac Do Lodge. Campers were assigned to cabins by age, but for activities, campers of all ages were divided into teams with names designating Indian tribes. These groups competed with each other in swimming, tennis, archery, and horseback riding. We also did crafts, and campfires where we sang and told stories. I loved it all.

The program was a perfect blend of competition and comradeship. My campmates elected me Chief of our tribe for my three years at camp. I made friends, loved the counselors and relished every moment. The last summer I was at camp, my happiness was shattered when I learned that my beloved Aunt Rae had died. My mother did not want to spoil my summer, so she did not bring me home for the funeral. In terms of my well being, that was probably a poor decision.

The summer after Daddy died, my grief-stricken mother wanted me with her, and did not want me to go back to camp. I was crushed and felt guilty because I wanted to return so badly. Later that summer, I got an invitation to drive to camp with parents of one of my friends for Visiting Day. Mom agreed to let me go. I was so excited, I couldn't sleep for nights. I got to see my friends at my favorite place on earth. When it was time to leave for home late that afternoon, I was heartbroken.

There was a camp rule that campers had to stay for the entire eight-week session, with no exceptions. Imagine my delight when Mac, the camp director asked me if I wanted to stay for the second four weeks. Oh boy, did I ever want to stay! When I called home for permission to stay, my mother sounded very sad. It was obvious she wanted me to come home, so I returned. My 15-year old soul was tormented on the ride home, as I fought back bitter tears of self pity, accompanied by a large dose of guilt for not wanting to go home.

A milestone event in every kid's life is learning to drive. My dad was still alive, so I must have been about 14 years old. There were no driver's training classes back then. Daddy knew a guy named Leo, reputed to be an excellent instructor. He exceeded his reputation. I learned to drive in no time, and loved my classes with him. He was kind and patient and made me laugh. Cars in the 1940s did not have power steering or automatic transmission, so I learned to shift gears. There was a clutch pedal next to the brake which had to be depressed with the left foot every time the gears shifted. Leo's best advice to me was, "When in doubt, both feet to the floor!"

I got my driver's license at sixteen. One day, I wanted to impress my favorite teacher Miss Kacharubus, who taught Spanish. She was young and fun and all the kids loved her. I asked Mom if I could drive the car to school. After the obligatory lecture to be careful, she gave me her keys. I knew Miss Kacharubus was planning to take the bus to East Chicago after school, to catch the South Shore train to Chicago, but I wanted to give her a ride to the station. Feeling important when she accepted my offer, I asked a few of my girlfriends to come along. After school we all piled in the car. We were all laughing and having a great time. As we approached a busy intersection, I was busy talking and did not notice the light had turned red. I did my "both feet to the floor" routine. The car slowed down but did not come to a full stop until it "touched" the car ahead.

Panic struck. Neither car was damaged, but I realized I might not have my license with me. Certain the driver would call the police, I panicked and took off! I was determined not to get caught, or cause my teacher to miss her train, so I kept going, avoiding main streets. Somehow, I managed to elude any imaginary or real pursuers. It was my most daring and stupid act since I had jumped from our roof to the next building.

Poor Miss Kacharubus -- I had put her in an untenable situation. I felt guilty about hitting the car, and even worse that I had committed the cowardly act of running away, but, at least, my teacher made her train. To my everlasting amazement and gratitude, Miss Kacharubus did not report me to the school or the police. But I had to face my mom with the gory details. I recall not getting the car again for a long time.

There are certain historical events that one never forgets. One event for my generation was December 7, 1941, Pearl Harbor Day, the beginning of America's involvement in World War II. All Americans old enough to remember that day can tell you what they were doing when they heard the news of the surprise attack on Pearl Harbor. I was 10 years old, and planning to go to a birthday party in Chicago: lunch, followed by a movie.

The mothers talked in the morning and decided not to spoil the party, so they did not tell us we were at war until we got home. I remember being very scared.

Although the war in Europe had been raging since 1938, the American people were still negative about getting involved in 1941. Pearl Harbor Day changed that. Japan's attack on our Navy, at a huge cost in American lives, energized the American people to enter the war. America's participation helped ensure the defeat of Hitler and saved our country from Japanese devastation. Historians have written that World War II might have been lost had America not entered the war when we did.

Nathan Kaufman, World War II Plane Spotter

The surprise allied invasion of northern Europe, known as D-Day (nearly four years after Pearl Harbor) precipitated Hitler's defeat. American and British troops moved across Europe from the west as the Russians were moving toward Berlin from the east. The Third Reich had bitten off more than it could chew when Hitler attacked Russia. Even when defeat was inevitable, Hitler accelerated his war against the Jewish people. He was determined to complete his goal of ridding Europe and the world of Jews. He continued to transport in cattle cars every Jew he could still find alive, to be gassed in the death camps in Eastern Europe. There have always been atrocities in human history, but never on the scale of the Holocaust. I agree with some scholars that this event was the result not only of Hitler's madness, but of thousands of years of anti-Semitism culminating in genocide so well organized and fanatically driven that it almost succeeded. When the war ended, one third of the world's Jews -- men, women and children – were mercilessly murdered.

To this day I am haunted by the Holocaust, and what I believe to be its relationship to European anti-Semitism. Hitler's maniacal war against the Jewish people had a tremendous impact on me. I learned to abhor bigotry and prejudice of any kind. This motivated me to dedicate lots of my volunteer and leadership efforts to bringing people of different ethnic, religious and racial backgrounds together. In college, my favorite volunteer activity was participating in the Panel of Americans, a group of students that accepted invitations to speak at university and community events. Four of us would go together, a Protestant, a Catholic, a Jew and a Black, to talk about our experiences for 10 minutes and then take questions.

Growing up in Indiana Harbor, I had a number of personal anti-Semitic experiences. In eighth grade, I was surrounded on the playground one day by a group of hostile girls. I think they were all black kids. They perceived themselves as poor and disadvantaged and saw me as a member of the privileged class. Their remarks were nasty and anti-Semitic. My family was considered middle class. I had more than they, but the Jewish "thing" really upset me. I told them I was sorry for their pain, but I was quite forceful in disparaging their racial remarks. I did not report the incident, and they never bothered me again. That experience had a lasting effect and taught me that bigotry and xenophobia were evil.

I became passionately committed to fighting racism in every way I could. Being on the Panel of Americans afforded me an official and powerful opportunity to assert my beliefs, and also talked about Judaism, a subject I was knowledgeable about. I believed the Panel accomplished its goal of reducing mistrust and hatred, and I found the work enormously satisfying. The Holocaust also taught me that the Jewish people have always been vulnerable, that Jews have had a painful history, and that we needed the State of Israel. Like so many, I have committed myself to working my entire life to help sustain the Jewish people, the State of Israel, and the rich heritage that is mine.

Many Jewish people stopped believing in God after the Holocaust. They could no longer believe in a God that would allow such cruelty. I went through many periods of doubt myself, but it seemed to me then, and still does, that most evil in our world comes not from God but from human behavior. Even the Holocaust cannot destroy my faith in the capacity for love in the human heart. To be human fosters a deep-seated need to believe that there is more to life than we can understand by reason alone. Judaism provides a standard of behavior and a belief system for me that celebrates life, requires no dogma, and does not challenge reason, but insists that human beings have a responsibility to partner with God in repairing a broken, imperfect world. My mind and my heart find no fault with that belief.

The war finally ended in 1945, with the surrender of Germany in May, and the surrender of Japan in August. A controversy remains. Many historians believe that had President Truman not used the atomic bomb, the war would have lasted much longer. America would have had to send ground troops to fight a land-battle in Japan at an enormous cost of our soldiers. Others argue that the enormous number of civilian deaths resulting from the use of two atom bombs made the President's decision immoral.

President Roosevelt's liberal New Deal helped to end the Depression, and his mobilization of the American people following the attack on Pearl Harbor made Hitler's victory impossible. Roosevelt was a hero to most American Jews. When he died in his unprecedented fourth term, my father was grief stricken. Working in the store when the news was announced on the radio, he rushed upstairs to tell my mother. Distraught and weeping, he put his arms around her as if to hold himself up and said, "Gertie, the President is dead."

About one year later, he came up those same 26 stairs for the last time. It was May 2, 1946. He had not been feeling well for the past year. I'm not sure what his symptoms were. Perhaps I forgot, perhaps no one told me. I remember that my mother took him to specialists in Chicago and the Mayo Clinic as well, but no diagnosis was made. He was working in the store when he started vomiting. He was in pain, decided to come home, and climbed the stairs to lie down on my bed. Mom sent me to get the doctor, whose office was next door. He arrived in minutes with his little black bag. When he came out of the bedroom a short time later, he told us Daddy was dead. I didn't cry, and I don't think I felt anything.

I have been tormented over the years thinking that if someone had called the doctor before he came up those difficult stairs, his heart could have made it through the heart attack. It was one week away from my 15th birthday. Mom was inconsolable. Even before Daddy died, I do not think she was a person at peace with herself or her world. Her grieving was beyond natural. I believe this stress and grief destroyed her immune system and precipitated her breast cancer from which she died on August 15, 1948, just two years later.

I think I was in denial for many years upon losing my parents. I'm not sure to this day that I ever came to terms with my losses. It did not help that people in those days did not discuss death and dying. It remains very painful for me that no one told me my mother was dying. When they finally took her to the hospital at the end, I was told nothing, and when the call came, I was in Chicago at my Aunt Frieda and Uncle Arthur's apartment. I'm not sure anyone was with my mother when she died. I hope Uncle Arthur was. I never got to be with her at the end. I am still troubled that I never really got to know her. If she were here now, there would be so many questions, so much to talk about.

It was after Mother's funeral that Aunt Frieda and I took the train to Eagle River, Wisconsin, where Irving had been at camp for the summer. It was my assignment to break the unbelievable news to my seven-year-old brother that his mother died. I don't know how I got through it, but I did. The decision to send him to camp was probably made by Frieda and Arthur and maybe by Ada and George as well. They knew Mother was dying and were trying to protect him from what they knew would be a difficult summer. Today, society is more enlightened about the importance of being forthcoming with children about terminal illness. But given the times, they were doing the best they could under unbearable circumstances. I only remember there were a lot of adults whispering that summer, and people would stop talking when I entered a room. I guess I was too afraid to ask questions. I believe that is called denial.

After our parents died, Irving and I remained in our home. It was to be my senior year in high school, and I did not want to move. I wanted to stay in Indiana Harbor until I graduated, even though Aunt Ada and Uncle George were willing to take Irving and me to Terre Haute, Indiana to live with them. Irving could have gone, and probably should have, but Uncle George told me my mother had insisted that Irv and I not be separated. That normal motherly request, given the big difference in our ages and hence in our individual needs, turned out to have created immediate and ravaging problems for both Irving and me.

I learned later that Minnie, Uncle Duke's wife, who coveted our flat above the store, spoke openly about wanting to move in after Mother died. In fact, she couldn't wait until our mother died. She finally got what she wanted. After the funeral, she and Duke and their two children moved in with us. Minnie treated Irving and me shabbily. It was an excruciating year, and we hated her. She was hostile and cruel. To make matters worse, our uncle was putty in her hands.

Irving had been given a special honor at our synagogue. Rabbi and Mrs. Kahn had invited him to participate in Shabbat services in kindness to him, and maybe to get more people there. Since the entire Jewish community in Indiana Harbor had known and loved our parents, there would have been a huge turn out at Shabbat services, but it never came to be. I can't remember what Irving did that week to infuriate Minnie, but I vividly remember what she did to punish him. She canceled his appearance that Shabbat. I pleaded with her. Lots of people called her. I remember my stomach was in knots and I despised her. Finally, I took my uncle aside. I was crying when I said, "Uncle Duke, you have to make her let Irving do his part at shul. He's just a little boy. She is being very mean to him." He said he would try, but when nothing came of it, I lost all respect for him. As far as I was concerned, he was her accomplice in crime.

Things went from bad to worse. Whenever Irv got mad, he would let Minnie have it, but I kept everything in. One Friday night in February, I had a date to see

"Finian's Rainbow," a popular and very beautiful musical, and I looked forward to the evening. The show was great, but I wasn't. I got very sick at the theater, and my date had to bring me home. I was up all night with terrible cramps, diarrhea and rectal bleeding, but Minnie was annoyed because I kept her up, too. She wanted to go to Chicago the next day with her daughter Natalie. As sick as I was, they went anyway. As the day progressed I got worse and finally called my Aunt Frieda and Uncle Arthur in Chicago. They picked me up and took me to the Wesley Memorial Hospital, a part of Northwestern University Medical School. The doctors thought I had a bowel obstruction. I had a high fever and a white blood cell count of 23,000. Surgery was seriously considered.

While the Red Sea did not part, a small personal miracle did occur that night. When the doctors were debating my fate in the middle of the night, the bleeding lessened as did the diarrhea. So instead of emergency surgery, I was put on painful penicillin shots in my backside every four hours around the clock for the next 10 days. My white count came down, and I was finally released from the hospital but warned not to go back to Minnie and Duke. The doctors were convinced that stress brought on my illness.

My father's cousin and his wife had been good friends of my parents. Aunt Evelyn and Uncle Nate, who had two daughters about my age, invited me to live with them for the next two months until I graduated. Everyone urged me to do so, but Irv remained in that hell hole. I felt guilty about leaving him after my illness, but I was still weak and terrified to go back. So he and I remained in Indiana Harbor. I would pick him up on Friday as soon as I got out of school and head for Chicago to spend the weekend with Aunt Frieda and Uncle Arthur. When graduation day finally arrived, we had the car packed with our belongings. As soon as the ceremony was over, we left Indiana Harbor.

Except to visit the graves of my parents, I have rarely gone back to the little town in which I grew up. When I left after commencement, I hoped I was severing forever that part of my life. Needless to say, this entire episode was an excruciating experience for Irving and me. Why Irv remained with Minnie and Duke after I moved out and did not immediately go to Terre Haute to live with Ada and George will forever remain a mystery. There is no one left I can ask about this. My assumption remains that the family still felt bound by my mother's wish that we not be separated.

That summer Aunt Ada and Uncle George adopted him, and Irving moved to Terre Haute to begin a new life with his new mom and dad. I was sent to New York for a month to stay with Margie, Aunt Frieda and Uncle Arthur's married daughter.

Many years later, Irv and I went on a pilgrimage to Indiana Harbor. My daughter Gayle came with us. On the long ride from Detroit, I told them lots of stories and tried to reveal those memories and experiences with a lighter side. Lots of them included Irv, who was grateful to hear about our family life. He had been so young when his parents died, he had forgotten a lot of his past. We stopped at the cemetery where our parents are buried in Portage, Indiana outside of Gary. I brought a prayer book along so we could say Kaddish, and we recited Psalm XXIII. The gesture was a healing experience for us. The biggest shock was returning to Main Street where I lived from about 1936 to 1949. Indiana Harbor was a ghost town. Main Street looked like a war zone. It appeared that people were living upstairs in our flat, but I did not have the stomach to put myself, Irving and Gayle through a tour, so we didn't knock on the door. Instead, we looked at what was left of the Kaufman Hardware Store. The tile floor which covered the entry to the store was chipped and ugly, but the name "Kaufman" was still imbedded in the broken tile. There was really nothing left of its former loveliness. It was empty and desolate—as were the three of us. The trip was difficult. By the time I got to Chicago, my stomach was churning, and I lost my appetite. I was relieved to get back to Detroit.

I had been a reasonably happy teenager when my parents died, but only reasonably. Some of my issues had begun long before I lost my parents. I had always been a nervous child, and felt as though I were two different people in one. There was the jovial, fun-loving extroverted Jessie, for whom relating to people was a necessary and positive experience. Another, more secret part of me struggled to be positive and had many doubts about my authenticity. In retrospect, I think I was a classic case of a neurotic child. I did not know how to integrate the two Jessie's, and only now, at age 78 am I beginning to understand and deal with some of the issues which formed me.

When I was about 14 years old, a 20-year old soldier, Mickey Feltenstein, was visiting his sister, Frieda Goodman, in Indiana Harbor. I can't remember the circumstances of our first meeting, but he had a crush on me. He was very attentive, and always a perfect gentleman, but my mom and dad were uncomfortable because of the age difference. Mickey invited me to a dance, and in typical fatherly fashion, my dad insisted on driving us to and from the event. It was fun to be on a pedestal. When I went away to college in the fall of 1949, he asked to marry me.

Aunt Frieda elected herself to take charge of my life after my mother died. She was a powerful lady who offered me love and sometimes even good advice, and she liked Mickey, too. She thought he would make a good husband and urged me to consider marriage. Aunt Frieda had a strong hold on me, and I rarely crossed her. Her love was conditional, to receive it, I had to toe the mark -- her mark! I was needy and went along with most of her suggestions and demands, but somewhere, somehow, in the case of Mickey, I found the inner strength to do what was right for me.

EXODUS

"Yeziat"

The first week I was in Bloomington during my freshman orientation in 1949, I met a guy. His name was Shelly Stern. While I was living in Terre Haute the summer of 1949, I had a few dates with Eddie Allen, a ZBT at Indiana University. He told his frat brother, Sheldon Stern that he met a cute gal who was coming to I.U. and suggested he should call me. In those days, Coca Cola dates were an inexpensive and popular blind date method. So on a fateful afternoon in early September, Shelly called and we arranged to meet in front of the library. We walked across the street to The Gables, a popular campus hang-out reputed to be the place where Hoagie Carmichael wrote *Stardust*.

My first impression of Shelly was positive, but it was hardly love at first sight. He was polite, intelligent, considerate and cute looking. We spent a few hours together, and I had a good time. A couple of days later he called again. We dated lots during my freshman year. The more I got to know him, the more I admired his many fine qualities. He vied for my time with Harry Sobel, his frat brother, and Jerry Pryweller, a "Sammy," another Jewish fraternity. Jerry had a Studebaker, a very sporty car. Shelly would often say to me, "That Pryweller has a 4 wheel personality!"

Shelly was my hands down favorite. We enjoyed each other's company. When the dorms and fraternity dining rooms were closed on Sunday nights, Shelly would often take me for an elegant dinner at the Union Building. I remember the white table cloths and excellent service, and I felt like a princess. If my friends were taken out at all, they would most likely report on their dinner at the Gables, or other such undistinguished places. It did not take long to realize that I had met a "winner." I remember often saying to myself that first year, "Shelly is the kind of person I would like to marry, but I'm just not in love."

Happiness is young love, Jessie and Shelly, circa 1949

At the end of my freshman year, Aunt Ada and Uncle George took me in for the summer. It was convenient living in Terre Haute with them and Irv, since Shelly had decided to apply to medical school and had some required science classes to take. Shelly drove to Terre Haute, an hour's drive from Bloomington, every weekend. On one memorable date early in the summer, we were sitting in the car saying good night. As he usually did, Shelly leaned over to kiss me good night. That's when "it" happened. I felt something had exploded in my head. No, it must have been in my heart. Unexpectedly, that kiss was different! At that moment I learned what "falling in love" meant. I was smitten beyond repair -- suddenly and irreparably, madly in love. We held each other tightly, and I could barely let go of him. There were bells ringing as my pounding heart opened to engulf this new and glorious experience.

I was overjoyed by the turn of events of that fateful summer night of 1950 when I was smitten for life by love. That summer was ablaze in love. We had tons of fun, played golf, went to movies, talked and talked and talked—and kissed a lot. In those days most people in love did not have sex unless they were married. We had a sentimental and very committed romance, and I believe we started talking about getting married, which necessitated introducing him to Aunt Frieda and Uncle Arthur. They were duly impressed by his character, thoughtfulness and charm, but they still hoped I'd marry a Jewish millionaire.

I should not have done it, but with their encouragement, I went to summer school at the University of Wisconsin in Madison in 1951. I dated a little. In fact I met Eddie Loeb. He was very rich and his parents owned a large department store in Lafayette, Indiana. Eddie was cute and nice, but from my "in love" point of view, he did not light a candle to Shelly. I spent most of my time summer writing letters to Shelly. He drove to Madison at least once and we both knew we were still meant for each other. I left Madison before the semester ended to be with him.

When I returned from Madison, we drove to Brown County State Park, a gorgeous park about an hour's drive from Bloomington, on a perfect summer day. When we parked the car near a little lake to take a walk, we discovered a row boat tucked under a bush at the shoreline. "Look what's waiting for us," Shelly said. We grinned at each other, climbed in and pushed off. About a half hour later we were still talking about what a gorgeous day it was and how much we loved each other. Shelly stopped rowing. Tiny waves were gently lapping on the bow. The conversation became more intense, followed by a moment of stillness. Then with tears in our eyes, we both, simultaneously, expressed the desire to get married as soon as possible. The boat, the lake, the sky and indeed the entire universe vibrated with our love for each other.

Jessie's Engagement Photograph

Soon, Shelly's folks and Frieda and Arthur met in Chicago to celebrate our engagement. I gave Shelly a beautiful Patek Philippe watch engraved on the back with his name and date of our betrothal, July, 1951. Aunt Frieda got it for me from a jeweler friend in New York. I paid $300 for it, which was a lot of money for me to spend. Today it is worth about $10,000.

Shelly's folks were less than enthusiastic about our engagement. His mom had other plans for him. She wanted him to marry a wealthy gal from Fort Wayne whom he had dated in high school. No wonder she and my Aunt Frieda got along. They shared the same values. My future mother-in-law did not hide her disdain for me; nonetheless, the Sterns bought Shelly a smashing 2.6 emerald cut diamond engagement ring to give me. We were both bowled over, and the two families hit it off. Shelly's mom took me aside and said, "You have a beautiful family." She was referring to their good looks. It was the nicest thing she had said to me since I met her a year before.

We decided to get married during Christmas vacation in 1952, but we got impatient and moved the date to Thanksgiving, November 27. It was my senior year, and Shelly was a junior in medical school. As an aside, you should know that when Shelly applied for medical school, he did not think he would get in. But I was confident. I will never forget when he got his acceptance letter, he was almost in tears when he jubilantly announced, "Jess,

Jess, they let me in! Can you believe it? They let me in." Not only had they "let him in," they *let him* begin after his third year as an undergraduate student, so he was able to get his undergraduate and medical degrees in seven years.

Our wedding was extremely emotional. We were married in Aunt Frieda and Uncle Arthur's beautiful apartment with a lovely view of Lake Michigan. Rabbi Kahn, my Indiana Harbor rabbi officiated. There wasn't a dry eye at the event. Shelly cried so hard during the ceremony, I wasn't sure he wanted to be there! Most of the tears were shed by relatives on my side of the family who were thinking of my dear parents. They would have rejoiced at their daughter's marriage, and they would have adored Shelly.

Cutting the cake at our wedding with Frieda and Arthur and Shelly's mother and father, Mary and Sam Stern

Jessie (Kaufman) and Dr. Sheldon Stern, November 27, 1952, Chicago, Illinois. Rabbi Eli J. Kahn officiated.

Following the ceremony, Aunt Frieda and Uncle Arthur hosted a traditional and delicious Thanksgiving dinner at the Belmont Hotel. We both had to be back for class Monday morning, so the honeymoon was brief. We stayed at the Edgewater Beach Hotel, a landmark hotel on the shoreline of Lake Michigan. Our room was beautiful. My adorable grandfather, Nathan Kaufman, was also at the hotel. We spent time that weekend with him. To this day Shelly still tells people. "Can you believe it? On my honeymoon I had to eat with Jessie's grandpa."

But that's only part of the story. Shelly's mother asked us to drive his sister back to Bloomington where she was also a student. Mind you, those were precious hours in that car. When Shelly and I parted in Indianapolis, I continued on another 60 miles with Beverly to Bloomington, very much aware that Shelly and I would not see each other until the next Friday. For newlyweds, those five days seemed like an eternity.

Friday finally came, and I drove back to Indianapolis to renew our married life together for the weekend, a cycle that continued for the next four months until I finished my classes and thankfully began student teaching in Indianapolis. Fortunately, I did not get evicted from the SDT House after I got married. The sorority had a rule: no married sisters were allowed to live in the House, but thankfully they made an exception for me. When I got back from Indianapolis on Sunday nights, I got lots of looks and a few smirks as my sisters asked, "Well, Jessie, did you have a good time?" I would smile and tell my mostly virgin sorority sisters that I had a great weekend!

With Shelly's encouragement, I got active in campus activities. I had been a good student and leader in high school, but really blossomed at I.U. By senior year, I was well known by students and the campus administration. The crowning glory was being "tapped" as a Mortar Board. Twenty women were selected from each senior class based on scholarship, leadership and service. We were an awesome group in 1952-53. I was elected president by my peers in a very close election. We did a number of worthwhile projects for the university, and have had three reunions over the years.

Shelly and Jessie, Presidents of Indiana University Hillel, with Rabbi Albert Yanow, Director, March 4, 1951, presenting an award

I.U. was a first-rate university, and I believe I received a first-rate undergraduate education, majoring in speech and hearing therapy. But of all the courses I took, the humanities excited me the most. I became a budding intellectual, and graduated in June 1953 with a 3.8 average (4.0 was straight A's). Not bad for a kid from East Chicago!

THE PERIPATETIC STERNS

"Navadeem"

We had a one-bedroom apartment in downtown Indianapolis on Vermont Street. At one time, it had probably been an upscale address, but it was obvious that the original apartments had been divided into smaller ones. Our kitchen could be described as a "hanging on the wall" variety. About six feet across, it opened onto a small living/dining room. Our bedroom was at the rear of the apartment. Our bed was near the back door, where we woke every morning to the sound of the janitor emptying garbage cans. This was a blessing in disguise, because it woke us up about 6 a.m., just in time for Shelly to throw on his pants and run outside to feed the parking meter. A motorcycle cop was usually waiting nearby to give us a ticket. Sometimes, Shelly did not make it in time and the tickets began accumulating. The police knew Shelly's Fort Wayne address, which directed the tickets to his Dad's mailbox in Fort Wayne.

On one visit to Indianapolis several months after we were married, Shelly's dad presented a thick envelope of tickets out of his breast pocket to his son. We assured Shelly's dad that we had tried everything, but we could not afford to keep the car in a public garage. I said that I frequently snuck the car into the Indiana University extension parking lot, but was terrified I would get caught. I really hated ducking down so the guard on duty could not see me sneaking away. Poverty was not easy. Blessedly, Shelly's dad took care of the tickets.

Frieda and Arthur gave us a beautiful hand-painted bedroom set, which had been theirs. As newlyweds, we hated it. Not only was it old fashioned, but it had twin beds. It now occupies a place of honor in the guest room of our Franklin home.

I finally graduated in June 1953. That summer, I worked in the Hearing Clinic at the Indiana University Medical Center under supervision. I did hearing tests and worked on improving the speech of severely hard of hearing children. It was a wonderful learning experience. That fall, I started my job as a speech therapist in the Indianapolis Public Schools. My annual salary was a whopping $2,700. We were rich! Not really. We kept a budget and we accounted for every cent, including chewing gum which was five cents a package. Hamburgers at the White Tower were 10 cents. To make extra money, Shelly would sell a pint of blood for $25 at Methodist Hospital in Indianapolis. He also had a part time job as an extern in the lab where he worked, and became proficient at drawing blood. Whenever, I have had an IV over the years, I would tell the technician that my husband was the best IV tech at the Methodist Hospital in Indianapolis when he was in medical school. Most of the time, they would just smile politely. What did they know? I got this assessment from him!

We bought a drop leaf French provincial table and four chairs for $350. I made monthly payments of $37 in person at the bank to pay off the loan. We got our money's worth from that investment. When we moved into our Franklin home, the table and chairs graced our new dining room until we got our current set.

Since we did not have much money, it was a very big deal to go out for dinner. We found a sweet little Italian restaurant not too far from our apartment. It had red and white checkered table cloths, and an empty Chianti wine bottle served as a candle holder on each table. Very romantic, we thought. But the best part was the price: a plate of spaghetti with meatballs and a salad cost only $1.50.

One night we decided to splurge and go there for dinner. Shelly left to get the car and said he would meet me in front of the apartment. When I got outside, I saw a tall man dressed in a business suit standing at the curb with Shelly. They were having a heated conversation. I noticed a gun in the man's hand. My reaction was instinctual. I ran towards them crying, threw my arms around Shelly and said, "Oh, please don't shoot my husband. We just got married." The man looked surprised, tipped his hat to me and said, "I am a detective. Sorry, "Ma'am." He showed us his badge, walked to his car and drove away.

As he thankfully left, I asked Shelly what happened. He reported that as he was backing out of the building next door where he had parked our car, he inadvertently bumped the horn at the very moment the detective was walking across the driveway in front of our car. He mistakenly believed Shelly had honked at him on purpose. It scared him, made him angry, and he pulled his gun. My theory is that the detective had probably been drinking before he came out of the bar. Needless to say this event spoiled our much anticipated evening out.

Shelly wanted to report this guy to the police department. While I agreed that the detective's behavior was way out of line, I was afraid to report him. It was Shelly's senior year in medical school by then, and every second night he slept at the hospital. I thought, if we reported the detective, he would likely be disciplined by his supervisor, and if he got drunk again, he might come looking for Shelly with his gun, and I would be alone in the apartment. I finally won the argument, but Shelly was furious with me. There was no romance that night, just a huge argument.

Our first year of marriage was not easy. Shelly was working very hard at the hospital, still studying whenever he had a free moment. I was young, immature and needy. I hated being alone every other night. When he came home after 36 hours, he was exhausted and not very sociable. I wanted to talk and perhaps go out, but he just wanted to sleep. I felt more than a little sorry for myself, but we still loved each other tremendously and we got through it.

We lived in Indianapolis until spring 1954. After we celebrated Shelly's graduation from medical school, we moved to Cleveland to start his internship at Mt. Sinai Hospital. It was not our first choice but the pay was the best anywhere: $200 a month plus four free meals a day for Shelly when he was on duty. Most of the other good teaching hospitals paid from $25 to $50 a month. So we ended up in Cleveland for the next year. We found a one-bedroom apartment in Cleveland Heights, about 15 minutes from the hospital. I got a job as a speech therapist in the Cleveland Public Schools. I think I made about $3200 that year. Again, we felt rich.

Jessie and Shelly in their Cleveland Apartment

We became very good friends with Sibyl and Eddie Eigner. They were a darling newly-wed couple, and Eddie interned with Shelly. We had a great time together, and being friends with Sibyl made the internship easier for me. I wasn't as lonely as I had been in Indianapolis and actually got used to Shelly's schedule. When the guys weren't too tired, we would occasionally go out together. That was always a treat.

Left to right: Roger Newman, Jessie, Eddie Eigner, Sibyl Eigner, Judy Newman, Shelly, Roz Roginsky

One day we decided to go to the symphony with them, and I offered to get the tickets. One afternoon earlier that week, I headed for the Severance Hall box office, but did not get far when it started to snow. A few blocks later, I found myself in a blizzard. Visibility had become a problem and the streets turned icy, but I forged on. Severance Hall sat on a small hill on a pie-shaped lot. The entrance was off a driveway that could be accessed from two different streets. Because of the storm, I did not park my car, but left it on the driveway by the box office entrance.

I was just deciding whether to splurge on better seats when a distraught man came up to me and said, "Lady, *was* that your car out there?" I ran outside. My car was gone. By then about three inches of snow had accumulated. As I followed the tire tracks, I realized that I had probably forgotten to engage the emergency brake or put the car in park. Since the driveway was on a hill, my car started to roll.

I followed the tire tracks across the street, up the curb and, with only inches to spare, between a sign post and a tree, down a steep embankment and into the picturesque pond that fronts the famous Cleveland Museum of Art. My car had taken a nose dive. To my horror, the upended back of the car was all I could see peering out of the water. I was panic stricken.

My attention was suddenly drawn to a crowd gathering down the street. Some were looking at the car. Others were standing beside a car pulled up along side the curb about 20 yards beyond. I ran over to the parked car. The driver was an elderly gentleman who was white as a ghost. Apparently, he was driving along when he saw my car, which almost hit him, come out of the driveway. His immediate response was anger, but when he saw the car continue up the curb and descend into the pond, he was sure someone was trying to commit suicide. At that point, I conjectured, he nearly had a heart attack.

Reluctantly, I introduced myself and explained what had happened, apologizing profusely. By that time I was nearly in tears. Once I was sure the gentleman was recovering, my attention returned to the greater problem at hand. There was a small building beside the pond which was next to my upside down and very wet car. I needed a tow truck, and thought I could call from the building, which was the arboretum of the museum.

The next thing I remember was being questioned by a woman behind a desk. She was upset and hostile, and I knew that my ordeal was just beginning. She called the director of the museum, a famous art historian and scholar named Sherman Lee. Dressed in a herring bone overcoat with a black velvet collar, a Homburg hat and carrying a walking stick, he was a distinguished looking gentleman -- and extremely angry. "Young lady, do you realize that your car has damaged our very valuable Japanese bushes?" he said. "They will have to be replaced if they die." At that point I not only nearly died myself, but I finally started to cry. He left soon after, leaving the matter in the hands of the woman at the desk. The bushes must have survived because I never heard from him again.

The tow truck finally came, but getting the car out was a huge project that took several hours. After much discussion, they put a cable over a branch of a large tree and with the use of a pulley, eventually lifted the car out of the water and lowered it onto dry land. Of course, it was not drivable, and it was questionable if it would ever be. They towed it away.

By then it was dark out and still snowing lightly. I was alone with no wheels. I called Shelly, working a 24-hour shift in the Emergency Room and tearfully gave him the gory details, and asked him to come get me. His response stunned me. He said he could not leave the Emergency Room, and that I would have to walk to the hospital or take a cab. I said "THIS is an emergency!" I was furious.

By that time, the arboretum was closed, so I did not have access to a phone, and I did not want to spend the money on a cab. It was a scary walk through an unpopulated, dark and not that great neighborhood, but I made it. When I entered the doctor's dining room, I was greeted by laughter and applause. I was badly shaken and did not think what had happened to me was funny, but I got over my humiliation enough to have supper and even *kibbitz* with the gang. Sibyl Eigner drove me home that night.

Shelly called the garage only to learn the towing fee was $225 -- more than he made in a month. Luckily, one of his patients was the Chief of Police in Cleveland Heights. The Chief said, "I do business with those guys, I'll call them for you." He did, and we paid only a fraction of the original bill. Thank goodness for city politics. About four weeks later, we got our car back, dry and running. By then I was healing and was able to joke about my personal catastrophe. We told everybody that the car had only one problem -- it blew bubbles every time we honked!

Towards the end of Shelly's one-year internship, a serious decision had to be made. What to do next? It was clear that he wanted to specialize, but what specialty? Shelly considered obstetrics/gynecology, orthopedics, urology and pediatric cardiac surgery. He even wrote to a famous pediatric cardiac surgeon asking for an interview. Shelly never got an answer to his letter. To this day, Shelly continues to believe that the guy was an anti-Semite.

About that time Eddie told Shelly that the Ophthalmology Department at Western Reserve University in Cleveland had offered him a residency which included the Lancaster Course, an academic summer course at Colby College in Waterville, Maine. Following that was a second academic course at Harvard Medical School. The classes would be taught by the most famous doctors and professors in their respective fields. Shelly got very excited about this program and decided to try it even though he wasn't sure he would like ophthalmology. Because he had applied earlier than Shelly, Eddie was able to begin the clinical portion of the residency immediately following the residency. But Shelly needed to occupy himself in another endeavor before his clinical residency began. Fortunately, he was able to secure a position at the Massachusetts Eye and Ear Infirmary's prestigious Howe Laboratory, noted for its excellence in ophthalmic research.

Shelly applied for a $900 government grant to get us through the Lancaster Course. We were thrilled to learn we got it, but in typical government fashion we did not receive the money until September. We decided to rent a cottage with the Eigners for our stay in Waterville, Maine. For most of the journey we drove in tandem. It was quite an adventure.

The night before we arrived in Waterville, we found an old farmhouse with a sign, "Rooms for Rent—Vacancy". The farmhouse had an incredible gourmet dinning room. We were amazed. The four of us had a marvelous meal at a reasonable price. When it came time to check in, we were told they only had one room left with two twin beds! By that time it was late, we were tired and there was nowhere else close by. So we giggled, took the room and settled in for our first night of living together. We were all pretty embarrassed, but we got through it.

Over breakfast in our newly found gourmet restaurant, we scanned the local papers for available cottages to rent. We spent the morning looking at places which were all disappointing, but our luck changed later that day. We found a brand new furnished log cabin on

Lake Mesalansky with two bedrooms and a beautiful screened in porch right on the lake. Two brothers, probably in their twenties, had hand-built the place and were anxious to rent it. They were very sweet, promising us an ironing board and iron, a row boat and even a dock. How lovely.

But there was one embarrassing, but very serious, problem that required their urgent attention. We did not know whether to laugh or cry when Sibyl and I discovered the paper thin wall between the two bedrooms only went up two-thirds of the way to the ceiling. We blushingly told the brothers that while the ironing board, iron, boat and dock would be appreciated, what we needed the most and the quickest was a complete wall between the bedrooms. It was their turn to blush. The wall was finished the next day, and we moved in. The first item on each couple's agenda was to purchase a small radio for our hardly sound-proof bedrooms. The neighbors never complained that at odd hours of the night, strange music would waft out of the windows, but it was embarrassing to us. A week later, we discovered that taking long walks one couple at a time after dinner worked as well, and did not wake the neighbors!

The summer was delightful. Shelly and Eddie loved their classes. The professors were first-rate, and the subject matter engaged them both. Most evenings they studied, and we all spent a lot of time on our screened-in porch. There was no air conditioning, but the evenings were cool. The weather, the woods and the lake were reminiscent of my summers at camp in Wisconsin. Many years later I realized how similar Maine is to northern Michigan.

Sibyl and I worked out an equitable arrangement on sharing dinner responsibilities. We took turns. When one cooked, the other cleaned up. It worked pretty well, but I remember thinking that there were more dirty dishes and pots on the nights she cooked! The books were occasionally put aside to provide time for the couples -- together or separately -- to have some leisure time. Shelly and I fell in love with Gilbert and Sullivan that summer. The American Savoyards, a young, talented group performed in a little theater on a country road about 30 minutes from our cottage. We attended as frequently as we thought we could afford.

After a major discussion with the Eigners, we decided to buy a motor for our row boat. I caught a 3-lb. bass and a 2-lb. perch on different expeditions while motoring around our little lake. I could not have pulled the bass in if Shelly had not been on board to assist. The fish was so strong that he spun the boat in circles. But we persevered and finally won the battle. On both occasions we had the fish for dinner the night of our catch. And for each triumph I was interviewed by the Waterville newspaper and photographed with my fish, so there is proof of my fish stories!

We also explored the surrounding area, Camden and Bar Harbors, and found a wild blueberry patch behind the cottage. I think I made at least one blueberry pie. The summer was only marred by our increasingly desperate financial situation. By the end of the August we were literally broke. When Shelly's sister, Beverly, came to visit, she had about $100 with her when she arrived. She remained with us the last two weeks of our stay in Maine. When classes were over and it was time to return to Fort Wayne, we had to borrow $50 from Beverly to make it back to Shelly's folks' home. Thankfully, the grant money came in September. It seemed like a fortune. So ended the summer of 1955, and our adventure in Maine.

A few weeks later the Harvard class began, so we packed up and headed for Boston. The Eigners were there also, but this time we each had our own apartment. They had a one-bedroom place in a building with an elevator. I was jealous. We got a studio apartment on the fourth-floor of a walk-up building. The living room was so small that when we pulled the Murphy bed out of the wall, it filled the entire room.

Ah, but what a view we had. A lovely park was across the street, filled with roses. On the next block were victory gardens left over from World War II. The

Boston Museum of Fine Art, a beautiful neo-classical building famous for its American art collection was found on the far side of the park. We frequented the museum, and staked off a plot for our very own garden. It was fun growing vegetables the summer of 1956. Our neighborhood, which was less than snazzy, must have been quite exclusive at one time -- and no, we did not contribute to the neighborhood's decline!

We got used to our little place and settled down to our new life. We didn't have much money, but we knew how to have fun. Boston was famous for theater, and many of the shows that eventually made it to New York City premiered in Boston. If they got good reviews they would go on to Broadway. One day, Oscar Hammerstein stood next to us at the opening of one of his shows. We could get seats in the second balcony for $1.65, and often "splurged" to see some fine plays and musicals. We would tell our friends if they didn't mind an occasional nose bleed from the altitude, they should try it.

It was impossible to get tickets for the Boston Symphony. All of the seats were held by subscription. Some lovely older people we met at a temple during Shabbat services took a liking to us, and would often give us their symphony tickets when they weren't using them. We also discovered that symphony rehearsals were open to the public for a nominal fee. Our favorite was a concert conducted by Leonard Bernstein. I'll never forget the moment he walked out on the stage wearing a pair of khakis and a tee shirt with a towel around his neck. Since we were sitting in the third row, we could hear his comments to the orchestra. We also did lots of sightseeing in historic Boston and regularly took Sunday trips along the north coast to places like Gloucester and Marblehead.

A course on Medieval Jewish philosophers at the Jewish Community Center turned out to be a great idea. Our teacher was Rabbi Eliezer Berkovits -- kind, gentle, fun and an amazing teacher and scholar. He had been the Chief Rabbi of the Orthodox Community in Berlin until the Gestapo expelled him from Germany in 1934. He immigrated to England where he remained until he came to Boston at the end of the war. His impressive credentials also included a Ph.D. from Berlin University in Philosophy. He took a liking to Shelly and me. I started to attend Shabbat services regularly in his little shul in Newton, a Boston suburb. He would smile at me when he spotted me in the balcony. His sermons were terrific. He said he normally delivered his sermons in Yiddish, but decided to switch to English when I was there. His sermons were too good for such a small audience.

I spent many a happy Shabbat afternoon with his two teenage sons, and his bright and gracious wife, Salle. I learned a lot from him, and found my respect for Orthodoxy, which began as child, was enhanced by my contact with him. We corresponded for many years after Shelly and I left Boston. Rabbi Berkovits eventually moved to Chicago and taught at a major yeshiva in Skokie before making aliyah to Jerusalem. He wrote numerous books and published some astounding articles in noted Jewish periodicals. I also have cherished autographed copies of all of his books. I was thrilled one day when my current Talmud teacher in Detroit, Rabbi Rod Glogower, quoted from a book written by Rabbi Berkovits. He told the class he was a student of Rabbi Berkovits' at the yeshiva in Chicago. I may have made a few points with Rabbi Glogower when he learned I had once studied with Eliezer Berkovits. It's a small world we live in.

When Shelly and Eddie started the course at Harvard, Sibyl and I got jobs at the Massachusetts Heart Association doing menial clerical work for 50 cents an hour. It was very boring but we needed the money, and at least we were together. We brought our lunches to save money. When the Harvard course ended around the first of the year, Eddie went back to Cleveland to start his clinical residency. Shelly started his residency in September and got the job in the Howe Laboratory. He worked for Dr. David Cogan, a world famous ophthalmic neurologist. By the time we left Boston, Shelly had done the drawings for a new book Dr. Cogan authored. Not surprisingly,

Shelly is very proud of that. Until he died many years later, Dr. Cogan remained one of Shelly's mentors.

It was quite a year. The grant money was nearly gone, and I needed to find a better job. Months before, we had decided it was "time," and I had become pregnant. We were ecstatic. In the early months, I was not feeling great, but I applied for a job in the Lynn public schools system as a speech and hearing therapist. They needed someone mid-year. I had two strikes against me - I was pregnant and I would be leaving for Cleveland in the fall.

So I did not tell them and had to figure out how to conceal the pregnancy. I remember having a red suit which had a fulsome, boxy jacket which did the trick. They must have wondered towards spring why I wore the same jacket every day. When the skirt got too tight to zip, I used the largest safety pin I could find. It worked, and I made it through the spring semester. I finally told them I would not be back in the fall. Though, I still get a guilty pang about it, the truth is, that job saved us and made it possible for us to financially make it through our remaining months in Boston.

But our hurdles there were not over. A very hot summer began, and my due date was August 19. Shelly was still working at the lab, and we still lived in the fourth floor walk up on Riverside Drive. To minimize the stifling heat, Shelly opened the windows on the stairway landings up to our apartment to help circulate the air and allow us to sleep better. The next day, the landlord closed them. Shelly couldn't understand why he did that, so he opened them again. On the third day, when Shelly came home, the windows had been nailed shut, but Shelly pulled the nails out and opened the windows. That weekend, Shelly's folks had driven in from Fort Wayne to visit. Our apartment was barely big enough for Shelly and me, so they stayed at the Commonwealth Hotel.

As any good daughter-in-law would do, I invited them for breakfast. It was Sunday morning, and though the apartment was boiling hot, we were having a lovely breakfast. The landlord came running up the stairs and started yelling and swearing. He had discovered the nails removed and the windows opened, and pounded on our door. When Shelly opened it, he rushed in very angry, looked as though he was going to physically attack Shelly and told us to get out. I was terrified. Shelly's mom and dad helped us pack up, and we were gone. We even left the television! We had no place to go, so we moved into the Commonwealth Hotel. It was cool in there, but the hotel was expensive and with the baby due in three weeks, we did not know what to do.

When Shelly went to work the next day, he told Dr. Cogan what had happened. Dr. Cogan smiled and said, "My wife and I are going to northern Michigan for the month of August. We were hoping to find someone to house sit for us, and would be happy to have you move in." So we did. The house was in Belmont, Mass. I was a nervous wreck the whole time we were there, and constantly concerned that I could not take care of the house properly. It was huge. Just washing the kitchen floor was a gigantic undertaking.

I was not feeling that well, and the house was hot. I remember being lonely and apprehensive about having my first delivery. It was not a happy time for me. We still had the issue of where we were going to live when Dr. and Mrs. Cogan came back from Michigan. Then another miracle happened. Dr. David Donaldson, a younger man and one of Dr. Cogan's associates, knew Shelly and was aware of the bind we were in. He told Shelly that he and his wife were going on vacation when Dr. Cogan returned and we could use their house. The timing was perfect. Our Guardian Angel was alive and well—and alert!

On Friday August 17, a few hours after Shelly left for work, I felt something wet running down my leg. I sat down, called Shelly and heard him very excitedly say, "Oh my God, your water broke. Don't move! I'll be right home." He must have flown. I took a few minutes to pack a bag, and boom, he was there. We left immediately for the hospital. Shelly was sure it would be a short labor. By the time I was checked in I was starting to get a few contractions but nothing monumental. After a few hours, the nurses advised me to start walking the hall hoping to speed up the labor, but nothing much happened the rest of that day. By Saturday, I was getting discouraged and depressed. I was sure something was wrong with me. Again, nothing happened until about 11 p.m. on Saturday when I finally went into hard labor. I had no idea what to expect.

Though the Boston Lying-In Hospital was an eminently famous institution, part of Harvard Medical School, my experience there made it difficult for me to believe that they had made any advances in obstetrics since it's founding in the 18th Century. I was taken to a large labor room lined with beds filled with other women in hard labor. Most of them were carrying on loudly, each in a different key. They would not allow husbands in, so I was alone with a nurse in attendance.

I had a violent reaction to a drug they gave me and believe it totally dehydrated me and made me schizophrenic. I was pleading for water and thrashing around. They finally tied me down, including my legs. When the nurse finally brought me a wet wash cloth to suck on, I grabbed at it with my teeth, and heard the nurse scream. I had bitten her finger. That was the only moment of pleasure I had until 17 hours later when I opened my eyes to see Shelly's smiling face.

He was holding my hand and told me we had a very sweet and precious little girl, born at 4:10 Sunday afternoon. She weighed 4 lbs. 12 ounces and was perfect. She is still perfect! We named her Gayle after my mother, Gertrude. I was discharged from the hospital five days later, but Gayle Debra remained in the nursery for another week until she reached 5 lbs. We had set up a nursery in the Donaldson's living room with a darling bassinet. Gayle was so tiny she looked lost in it. Shelly's mom came to help me for a few days. The Donaldson's came home; Shelly finished his job at the Howe Lab; and we set out for Cleveland to begin the clinical portion of his residency at Western Reserve University. Blessedly, we were at last a little family.

We moved back into the one-bedroom apartment we had when Shelly was an intern, but neither of us can remember for sure how we got it back. It was fun but challenging being a new mom. Shelly was on call every third night, which meant he had to sleep at the hospital. Gayle was a long way from figuring out that night time was the time to sleep. The poor darling had colic, and she was probably allergic to the formula. The pediatrician never suggested that, so she and I, and Shelly when he was home, continued to suffer.

We weren't in Cleveland very many months when Shelly got drafted into the Air Force doctor's draft and learned that he would be sent to Japan for two years. Once again, our Guardian Angel was activated. Dependents were allowed to join their spouse overseas once housing was found for the family. We started praying that Shelly would find housing soon after he arrived in Japan. Also, while most doctors who were drafted did not get to pursue their specialty, Shelly was assigned as an ophthalmologist to a large hospital, a real bonus for him and two additional years of excellent training. Our other good fortune was that Shelly's sister's husband, Stanley Skilken, stationed at Pearl Harbor, was at sea at that time. Gayle and I needed a place to stay until Shelly found a house for us in Japan, so we moved in with Bev.

Our Air Force adventure began in February 1957, as we drove to Montgomery, Alabama for three weeks of Officer's Training School, where Shelly learned how to wear his uniform and how to salute. Then we drove to San Francisco, and he departed for Japan. We stopped at the Grand Canyon on the way. Anyone who has ever been there will tell you how truly awesome it is. Holding Gayle in my arms and looking at the spectacle before me was a religious experience that moved me to tears. She was only 6 months old, but I very carefully held her close to me and leaned over the wall to show it to her.

We stopped in Los Angeles overnight, and stayed with Aunt Frieda and Uncle Leo before tackling the last lap of our journey, the spectacular drive from L.A. to San Francisco. I was understandably apprehensive about the immediate future. For one thing, when we arrived in San Francisco, I dreaded embarking on the first plane ride of my life. This was before the era of jet flight, so I would be airborne for at least eight hours on the flight to Honolulu. I was not happy about parting from Shelly, since his duty as an U.S. Air Force Captain scheduled him to Japan. All we knew was that Gayle and I could not join him until suitable family housing was found, and I had heard horror stories of families being separated for up to six months.

USAF Captain Sheldon Stern in Japan

I survived the plane ride with Gayle, while Shelly followed the next day on a military flight bound for Japan. Thankfully, his plane stopped in Honolulu over night. After a sad goodbye the next morning, he left. I was heartbroken. Hawaii was very beautiful. The weather was perfect: temperatures in the 70's with a brief shower before the sun came out every afternoon. I saw many rainbows, which gave me hope.

Beverly and I got along beautifully, but I could never completely relax. Gayle was still having sleeping problems, and I was having worrying problems. When would I get to Japan? I still had to face my next much longer plane ride over the ocean. The worst part was the pangs of withdrawal with Shelly so far away.

I survived, but not easily. Gayle was not a happy camper either. She seemed uncomfortable before, during and after feedings. She cried a lot and was still not sleeping through the night. She was, however, growing and developing beautifully and when she wasn't uncomfortable, she was a joy.

There were other moments of great joy. The telephone call I had been waiting for finally came. Four weeks after he left, Shelly called me excitedly and said, "Honey, I found a house. You can come."

Jessie and Gayle in Japan

I left a few days later on a large propeller plane that had been converted from a war materiel carrier. It was huge, noisy and uncomfortable. Gayle hated it, too. About 24 hours later, we landed in Japan. After a tearful reunion, I realized I was in a state of exhaustion. I found myself in a strange and exotic place on a gray day in the middle of Japan's winter. It was cold and dreary, and I had the first of several meltdowns. Poor Shelly.

He was so happy to have me there and had planned a special welcome for me. He couldn't wait to show me around Tokyo which was huge, noisy and teeming with humanity. I just wanted a bed. Instead, my darling exuberantly said he had a surprise for me. For my first night in Japan, he got a room in a Japanese inn with authentic furnishings, complete with tatami mats.

It was lovely, but when I asked where the bedroom was, his face fell. "Honey, there are no bedrooms in Japan. They sleep on futons on the floor," he said. "In the morning they roll them up and the room becomes their living room again". The futon was more like a mattress cover than a mattress, but at least they had a crib for Gayle. When Shelly took me in his arms and kissed me goodnight, I floated to sleep on my futon.

The next morning, after another brief walk around Tokyo, we left for our new life in Nagoya, about a 200-mile trip. Our car had been shipped overseas and was waiting for us. With a car bed on the back seat, a map and a full tank of gas, we were off. We were told that the road to Nagoya was the main highway in Japan, but the "highway" never materialized. Instead, we found ourselves on a dirt road with a lot of traffic, mostly motor cycles and three-wheel motorbikes pulling carts.

We went through village after village after village, where the houses literally came down to the edge of the road. Sometimes we could hardly see through the dust. I got more culture shock when I realized that people could live like that. Occasionally, we would get some relief and actually find ourselves in the countryside. I can't remember where we stopped to use the bathroom, or to get lunch. And changing Gayle's diaper was a real challenge.

Shelly thought he had the correct directions to our hotel at the foot of Mt Fuji, but as the day wore on -- like the "highway" -- the hotel never materialized. We were both getting nervous as the sun started going down. Shelly's Japanese vocabulary was limited, but he had memorized how to ask for directions. "Is this the road to Nagoya?" The answer was always given with a smile and a bow. "Hy, hy" (yes, yes.) It became dark a few hours later, and we knew we were lost. I had another meltdown.

Shelly was noticeably upset with the circumstances and with me. We REALLY needed to find a place to sleep. We came to a town about 10 p.m. and mercifully saw a sign for a hotel in English. We got a small western style room with a BED and a crib for Gayle. We found that we had driven to the wrong side of Mt Fuji. Mind you, I was annoyed with Shelly for not investigating the trip more assiduously before we started. Some dumb American told him it was not a bad trip, so I can't blame him for believing the guy.

Even on a Western bed, sleeping was not easy in the hotel. The sheets were like sandpaper. My arms were irritated and sore the next morning. But the next morning I squeezed around the bed, opened the curtains of the large window, and what I beheld brought me the first truly joyous moment I since I got Shelly's call in Hawaii. There it was, in all of its picture-perfect snow-capped glory: Mt Fuji. It was close enough that I felt I could reach out and touch it. The sun was shining, the sky was blue and after that incomparable million dollar view of one of the most famous mountains in the world. I felt I could tackle another day.

Mount Fuji, Japan

We got an early start and with my mountain still in view, we began the second day of our trip. About midday, after many "askings," I finally got the answer I prayed for when I queried, "Are we almost there?" There appeared to be a large city off in the distance. Shelly's answered, "Oh, my God, I think that's Nagoya. See that large TV tower? This is it!" Nagoya was home to the largest TV tower in Japan. We were there.

Shelly raved about the house he had found for us. It had two bedrooms, an American style kitchen, and he was sure I would love it. With that assurance, I breathed a sigh of relief as I started observing the environment of my new city. We spent at least 30 minutes driving through one highly industrial area after another, and I asked Shelly when we were going to get to a residential section. About that time he turned down an unpaved side street, pulled up to a little house, smiled proudly and said, "This is it." I then realized there were no residential neighborhoods in Japan. Houses and industry were side by side, and our house was between a blacksmith shop and another residence.

Stern's Private Rental, Nagoya, Japan

At first I was in shock. The house was an attempt at Western style. It had the two bedrooms I was promised, indoor plumbing, and a small but adequate kitchen. The builders believed that all Americans were very tall, and made sure not to install the cabinets too low. I did not know whether to laugh or cry. I had to stand on a step stool every time I needed to reach even the bottom shelf. With no central heating, a pot belly wood burning stove warmed the living room, and the wood in the pot belly stove would die out shortly after we retired.

The night time temperatures in Nagoya often dropped to 32 degrees. We all slept in hats, and Gayle had mittens. That may be why I had to get her a pacifier.

Poor little darling could not find her thumb! When she smiled during a dream, I knew she was dreaming about the palm trees in Hawaii. And, poor Shelly had to get up every day at 5 a.m. to start the fire so the house would be at least a little warmer when we got up. He often had black smudges on his face when he got back in bed and snuggled up to me.

We were fortunate to have a maid, Shiziko San, who was sweet and very good to Gayle, so I was able to get out and meet people. I finally learned how to navigate: to drive on the left through the labyrinth of narrow streets, to deal with horrendous traffic, to find the commissary and the base hospital where Shelly worked. At least the hospital was warm! I felt liberated.

I finally snapped out of my funk and started meeting some of the other military wives and their doctor husbands and made lots of friends, many with who we are still in touch. Most of the other wives had been in Japan for a year or more. They were savvy and willing to share all kinds of tips. They were my salvation. I even learned to forget (well sort of) about the lack of a hot bath unless I went to a Japanese bathhouse where the water could scald you. We indulged in visits to a bathhouse only during occasional weekend vacations. Though we had indoor plumbing, the bathtub in our house was huge (no shower) and the water came out in a tiny stream and it was ice cold. It wasn't fun, but we did take baths every day—fast ones.

Our two-year stint in Japan flew by. We had a wonderful life there, with lots of weekend trips to the surrounding area and to Kyoto, a jewel of a city with beautiful shrines, gardens and a lovely little Japanese wood block print shop, which we frequented as often as we could.

We were transferred to the Tokyo area about six months after I had finally adjusted to Nagoya. This time, the adjustment was easier and brought many rewards, though it started off with a huge problem. The base housing we were promised was not available yet, so we lived in a hotel for about a week. There were always Japanese women in the hall wearing lots of makeup and very short skirts. All night long we heard doors slamming, laughter and squealing. The hotel was a "house of ill repute."

Things started to look up once we settled in Tachikawa. We had a full time, live-in housekeeper, Simi-San, who loved Gayle so much she didn't want a day off. She carried Gayle on her back, Japanese style. We were fortunate to make so many friends, to travel and to get many marvelous steak dinners, (with dancing) for $1.50 at the Officer's Club.

We were only 20 miles from Tokyo, where we satisfied our passion to collect blue and white porcelain, ceramics and Ukioye, which are old Japanese wood block prints. Shelly became quite scholarly over the 22 months of our tour of duty, and successfully assembled a noteworthy collection of Japanese treasures at a nominal cost. Many years later we donated most of the woodblock prints to the Detroit Institute of Arts and sold our blue and white porcelain and ceramic collections.

Shopping for Japanese artifacts for American service personnel was a way of life. Everyone shopped, but, Shelly and I distinguished ourselves with a reputation for going "all out." When our tour of duty ended, our friends made us a Sayonara Party. One comment at the party was, "Now that the Stern's are leaving, the curio shop owners have been overheard saying, 'We have to replenish our stock.'"

When we returned to the States, Gayle was two and a half, knew some Japanese and pronounced some of her English words with a Japanese accent. She was adorable. On our first visit to a supermarket, Gayle was sitting in the cart looking around. Suddenly, out of this tiny mouth a very loud voice came, "Oh, Mommy, what an "oki" (big) "commissorrry". The vowel was incorrect and she rolled her R's. Everyone in the supermarket rolled their eyes and laughed!

We left Japan, returning to Cleveland to finish Shelly's residency. I won't dwell on that part of our life, except to say that Jeremy was born there. After a miscarriage in Japan, we were really thrilled to have him. After three years, Gayle had a baby brother.

One day, Shelly excitedly came home from work. A doctor from Detroit had sent a representative to Cleveland to try to coax a professor to buy his Detroit practice so he could move to Boston. The professor loved his position in Cleveland. He turned down the offer and said, "I'm not interested, but I have a wonderful resident who is finishing up here in a few months. Why don't you talk to Shelly Stern?" Dr. Elmer Ballantine, I thank you from the bottom of my heart.

THE PROMISED LAND
Canaan

Moving to Detroit was huge and scary for us, with a permanence our previous moves lacked. The deal Dr. David Johnson made with Shelly was beyond our wildest dreams. After thoughtful consideration, Shelly and I agreed to "go for it."

Before we moved, we did not know anything about Detroit. We had heard of a lovely suburb named Grosse Pointe, which was reputed to be upscale and expensive. We took a drive out there one afternoon to explore, and discovered there were modest neighborhoods we thought we could afford. We stopped at a real estate office and the young man asked our name. When he heard our name, he stood up and said, "I don't think you would like it here." At that moment we realized anti-Semitism was alive and well in Grosse Pointe. We couldn't wait to get out of there.

When Shelly signed the deal with his future partner, Shelly picked up the pen to sign. Dr. Johnson turned to Shelly and casually said, "Oh, by the way, what religion are you?" Shelly was taken aback by the potential negativity of the question and remembered thinking this deal was too good to be true. He took a deep breath and said, "I'm Jewish." Johnson smiled. "That's wonderful," he said. "Now I can get you in the Jewish boat club. I'm the only non-Jewish member, and I will be happy to sponsor you." Shelly sighed with relief and said, "But I don't know anything about boats."

While looking for a place to live, we heard there was a new urban complex in downtown Detroit, a short distance from Shelly's office. It was three-bedroom townhouse in a co-op designed by Mies Van der Rohe. But having been burned in Grosse Pointe, we were afraid we might run into the same problem of anti-Semitism. Tom Watson, our agent showed us the unit and must have read our minds.

When we got back to Cleveland, Debbie Maxon, a colleague of Mr. Watson's, called to say she lived in Lafayette Park and that one of the many reasons she loved it there was that it was integrated. She also said she was Jewish. That did it! We decided we would love for our children to grow up in an integrated community. Lafayette Park became our new home. The Watsons and the Maxons became friends.

And joining the Great Lakes Yacht Club made it possible to meet lots of people during our first summer in Detroit and provided a fun place to spend our weekends as a family. Our dear friends, Ruth and Julian Lefkowitz, were among the first people we met that first summer at the boat club. We have remained close friends ever since.

In the fall, I wanted to meet more people and had heard of a Jewish medical society in Detroit with a strong women's auxiliary. They were having their first luncheon meeting of the fall season at the Wayne County Medical Society building, which was right across the street from Lafayette Park. So I dressed up in a suit and hat and white gloves, and at the appointed hour walked across the street.

Eleanor Lakin, an attractive young woman about my age, welcomed me at the registration table. She took me by the hand and walked me around to each table, introducing me to everyone. I sat at her table and had fun meeting other doctor's wives—who were all Jewish, too. Eleanor called me a few days later and suggested we make a date to go out to dinner with our husbands. And so began a life-long friendship. Eleanor died a few years ago from breast cancer. I was heart broken.

One more important decision remained; we wanted to join a temple. Shopping around, we attended services at the three Reform temples in town. Since Shelly was brought up in a classical Reform temple in Fort Wayne, we joined Temple Beth El. I got my nerve up again and attended a Sisterhood meeting, where a very accepting and friendly group of women introduced themselves to me. We joined the Married Group, once again enlarging our circle of acquaintances and new friends. In the meantime, David Johnson was introducing Shelly to lots of doctors. So we were getting off to a wonderful start in Detroit. We loved it then, and we still do.

When Lafayette Park opened a few years before we arrived, there was no public school, so the children got their education in a one-room school in one of the unoccupied units until a public school finally opened in 1961. The timing was perfect. Gayle turned five and was in the first kindergarten class in the new Chrysler School.

Our family grew. Our first Siamese cat, Sugar Plum was a smart little cat who would walk with me when I went to the little grocery store in our complex. Since I could not take her in the store, she would sit outside waiting for me. People were amazed. When she died, we got two more Siamese cats who were sisters Powder Puff and Penelope. Powder Puff was the runt of the litter, and it was touching to watch Penelope take care of her. She often lay on top of Powder Puff to keep her warm.

Walking to the Eastern Market with the kids every Saturday morning was a real "happening." Besides getting great bargains on fresh produce, residents of Lafayette Park congregated there for socializing as well as shopping. A lot was happening. We were active in the Married Group, Shelly was working hard, and his practice was growing. Life was good, but we wanted a real house.

Luck came our way again. We became friendly with Anita and Ralph Sosin in the Married Group study class. During the social hour one evening when the class was meeting at our town house, Ralph took Shelly aside and asked, "Would you and Jessie be interested in buying a lot in Franklin Village?" The lot was about two acres, part of a five-acre parcel for sale. The Sosins and the Zemans, their next door neighbors in Detroit, were looking for another compatible Jewish couple with young children to buy the third lot. At first, Shelly wasn't sure he wanted to see the lot, because it was so far from his office and there was no expressway. But curiosity and destiny won out.

The following Sunday, we piled the kids in the car and off we went to the Franklin Cider Mill. It took us about an hour to make the 20-mile drive. Though we had Ralph's directions, we weren't sure we could find it. We were on Franklin Road just past Thirteen Mile Road when Shelly slowed down, energetically saying, "Jess, Jess, I think this is it!" What we beheld was an ethereal meadow rolling up a large hill. We looked at each other in amazement, and my eyes brimmed with tears. We got out of the car, climbed the hill, and took in the beautiful view. Woods screened Franklin Road from the property, and the back of the hill descended, undulating until it fell away to bushes and trees. I was speechless! At that moment I felt a peacefulness descend upon us.

We drove through the charming old center of the village. At that point I had an attack of déjà vu. In a moment of poignant clarity, it all came back to me. I realized I had been there before! We had driven through Franklin Village four years earlier when we first came to Detroit, and took lots of Sunday drives, exploring Detroit and its environs.

Franklin Village, known as "The Town that Time Forgot" was founded in 1825. I was enchanted by the tiny commercial center of the town with its village green, colonial architecture and old cemetery with graves from the Civil War. I thought how fortunate the people that lived in Franklin were. It was such a special place. I could have never imagined that four years later I would be standing on that gorgeous piece of property that would soon be ours. It was inevitable that we should COME HOME to Franklin.

But on the way home, Shelly raised the same sobering points. Living in Franklin would be a long drive for him. And besides, we didn't have enough money to build a house. I realized he was as emotional and scared as I was, but in his usual rational manner he was trying to resist making a "leap of faith." It was true; we didn't have enough money to build a house, but could probably scrape together the $6,000 needed to buy the lot. I was scared, too, but we both succumbed, and the lot was ours. Shelly claims he did it as an investment, but I believe he wanted to live on that lot as much as I did. He still can't explain why he was compelled to drive to Franklin EVERY weekend to picnic with his family on his investment!

We started looking at model homes on a regular basis. The kids hated schlepping to the suburbs every week to look at models and to picnic on "the lot." We began talking about what we wanted our house–if we ever built it–to look like. We found ourselves returning to two models. We liked the first floor and exterior elevation of the Dutch Colonial model, and the second floor of the other model. With a few alterations we could combine the two floor plans. By taking advantage of the hill, we realized an exposed basement with two sliding doors opening to the back yard would work. The room could serve as a large party room, recreation room and play room for the kids. One night Shelly woke up about 3 a.m. He went to his desk and created drawings of the back elevation which included a screened-in porch and deck above the sliding doors below.

Less than a year later, we were driving around Franklin after Yom Kippur services, enjoying a beautiful fall day when I suddenly had an epiphany. With a full and pounding heart I said, "It's time! Shelly, let's do it." He felt the urge as I did. We smiled at each other, and so began the project of our dreams. We found a wonderful builder and by using Shelly's basic floor plan, we decided if we began immediately, there was time to start the house and get it enclosed before winter. It was a decision we have never regretted.

We broke ground sometime in early November and moved into our beautiful new home March 15, 1964. I think Wayne McBride, our builder, broke a record when he completed our house in less than four months. It was an extraordinary experience. We loved Wayne and were excited beyond description about the project and the prospect of living in Franklin on that hill in that house!

I think one of us drove out to the project nearly every day. We moved in without a blade of grass and no trees.

We were, literally, sitting on a sand dune. We planted grass seed. That first summer I dragged hoses up and down the hills and moved them every two hours. Shelly helped when he could, but he was busy growing his practice. By the end of the summer we had the beginnings of a lawn and started planting trees.

Home Sweet Home – after fourteen addresses all over the world – 26125 Woodlore Road, Franklin, Michigan

The first morning we woke up in our new place, we were having breakfast on our sand hill (All of the meadow grass had been destroyed by the building process.) Jeremy's classic remark that morning was, "Boy am I glad we don't have to go the lot today!!" After breakfast Shelly decided to neaten up our little estate by burning some of the boxes from the move. He dragged the empty boxes into a depressed area created by the digging. It seemed like a safe place, until the wind picked up and a spark jumped out of the pit, igniting the nearby weeds.

Within a few seconds a giant brush fire started racing toward the Sosin's house, two doors down. Shelly tried to bat the fire into submission, to no avail. I could see what was happening from the kitchen and called the Franklin Volunteer Fire Department. The fire fighters arrived before the fire could do any damage to Anita and Ralph's new house, but it did singe a few of their trees. I was more worried about Shelly, however. He had inhaled fumes and smoke and was coughing and spitting up phlegm for days. Every once in a while, the Sosins still ask him why he tried to burn down their house. And he reminds them that the fire was good for their trees, which survived and became healthy and beautiful.

The move to Franklin was not easy for Gayle and Jeremy. They had been nicely ensconced in our urban town house and were uprooted to begin a new life in a new school. It was particularly difficult for Jeremy. But they both eventually adjusted to their new life.

We decided to start buying American art. Once we started we were hooked. It became a passion and enhanced our lives. We made new friends, became knowledgeable and accumulated some real treasures.

Some of our paintings were shown in exhibitions as was our Alexander Calder mobile. We took a family trip to New York City for the opening of a Charles Burchfield retrospective at the Metropolitan Museum of Art, where we had loaned our Burchfield's painting, "Fallen Tree," to the exhibit. The kids still talk about the black tie dinner at the Met.

The Stern family at the Metropolitan Museum, New York City - dinner guests at the opening of the Charles Burchfield show with their painting, "Fallen Tree" dated 1954

Over the years we also donated a number of art works to the Detroit Institute of Art. When Shelly retired, we sold our art collection at auction in New York City for a considerable profit. By then Shelly had taken up painting, so I had lots of lovely things to replace our American art collection. The walls in our house are still covered with beautiful pictures by my artist in residence!

About 1983, Shelly decided he wanted to get a Master's Degree in art history, and enrolled at Wayne State University. He took one class each semester, with one interruption of a few years, until he realized his dream. It took unbelievable determination and dedication, but he finally got his degree. I tagged along, auditing a number of classes with him. It was a wonderful experience for both of us.

Shelly finally receives his Master of Arts in Art History from Wayne State University, Detroit, Michigan, December 1999. With granddaughter Emily Eubanks attending.

One day he came home from work and class and announced, "Jess, I have bad news for you. I have to go to Greece." He was taking a course in ancient Greek art and wanted to experience it first-hand. I was ecstatic. He knew he would not be going alone, so I got busy. Even though we couldn't afford the trip, I found some great deals which included a seven-day cruise of the Greek Islands and Turkey, plus four days in Athens. We went in late August. The weather was divine. It was a magnificent trip. Shelly's studies had paid off. Other honeymoon trips (we preferred going ourselves, not on tours) to Europe included several to our favorite country Italy, France and England.

I got increasingly active in the Jewish community. My two loves were the National Council of Jewish Women, and the Jewish Federation. I worked hard, made friends and felt I was contributing to society as well as to my own enrichment. In 1974, I became president of the Greater Detroit Section of NCJW. It was a full time job, difficult but rewarding. I went on to the NCJW national board, where I served for six years.

Jessie working the telephone for Jewish Federation of Metropolitan Detroit

A gathering of NCJW Presidents in our home

Jessie makes a Seder at our home for 32 people

Gayle graduated from Michigan State University in 1979 with a degree in Modern Dance, and immediately got a full time job with the Harbinger Dance Company in Detroit. She was a beautiful dancer and had a stellar career with Harbinger. Shelly and I found ourselves deeply immersed in the struggle to keep the company solvent. It was a huge challenge. From one pay period to the next, we were in a state of near panic, praying we could make the payroll. The struggle continued for years. There were times when I nearly gave up, but every time we went to a performance and the lights dimmed and the curtain went up, the struggle melted away, and Shelly and I found ourselves in heaven. Gayle's presence on the stage excited not only her dad and me, but the entire audience. She was a beautiful dancer and a true performer.

Another highlight of my years as a Harbinger volunteer was meeting and working with Ellen Pisor, general manager of the company. We laughed and cried together, and a wonderful friendship grew out our mutual love of dance and our determination to keep Harbinger afloat. In the bargain I became a pretty good fundraiser. Unfortunately, Lisa Nowak, the founder and gifted artistic director of Harbinger met an untimely death, and Harbinger had reached the end of the line. The company folded soon after.

About that time I decided something in my life was missing. I heard that the University of Michigan-Dearborn had a scholarship program for retired seniors. I enrolled and became a student again. I selected the humanities, which got my adrenalin going. The professors were marvelous, the classes were small and the students were a mixture of undergraduates and seniors like me. I especially liked the Honors Seminars which included a series on Western Civilization. In those classes we had two full professors. The learning and discussions were breathtaking. I continued taking classes for six years.

Shelly, meanwhile, got into collecting and restoring old cars. That turned out to be another life enhancing experience which could be best described as an adventure. In the fall of 1973, we were attending an Academy of Ophthalmology meeting in Dallas. We discovered a tennis court at a nearby high school. One morning we hopped on a public bus around 7 a.m. to sneak in a set of tennis before Shelly's meetings started. With no buses in sight when we finished, we walked to the nearest busy corner to hail a cab. None were in sight. As I continued my vigil, I heard Shelly in his most tender voice, say to me, "Look, Honey! Look at this."

I turned to see a black gravel lot filled with used cars. Shelly was pointing to a small car. We walked over to look, and I noticed its strange appearance. With small running boards, it looked like an antique. It was a Mercedes, built in 1952 when the Germans were still using pre-war molds reminiscent of a 1930's American car. For Shelly it was love at first sight. As in every love at first sight experience, the stricken one becomes obsessed with the beloved, needing her/it badly, and now! I had a big problem on my hands.

The next thing I knew, we were talking to a used car salesman, a creature of friendly and persuasive charm who even got me interested. When Shelly asked him what was wrong with the car, he replied with a big smile in his engaging Texas accent, "Oh, it has a bent rocker arm. Otherwise it's fine." He took us for a ride which was fun and soon the car was ours for $2,000. It was towed to Detroit with the plan that we would fix the rocker arm (whatever that was) and Gayle would use the car for transportation to and from school, freeing me up from my daily chore of driving her to school.

When the car we named "Junior" arrived, the "fun" began. We immediately had a serious problem. Junior wouldn't start. Shelly found a German mechanic on the east side of Detroit, a LONG way from our house, who found multiple problems. Junior was very sick, and according to the mechanic the only part of the car was that functioning properly was the rocker arm!

About three years, one rollover accident and $10,000 later, Junior was finally restored. Gayle had graduated high school, moved to Madison, Wisconsin and New York City and still did not have a car!! In spite of the cost and aggravation, we did have fun with Junior. He appeared in a show at Somerset Mall, metro-Detroit's most upscale shopping venue. It was not easy, but we eventually sold junior for $10,000, so we came out even.

Jessie and Shelly with "Junior" - a 1952 Mercedes Benz restored with the family's love for old cars

Our next old car venture occurred about 1980. Shelly wanted a classic car, which was defined as a car built from 1928-1947. He found a 1937 Mercedes in a garage in Hamtramck. Although the owner did not want to sell it, Shelly was persistent. One day he asked the gentleman, "If you ever decided to sell the car, how much would you ask for it?" He said, "About $5,000. Soon after the car became ours, and Shelly named our new challenge, "Senior," and had it towed home. When I saw it, I nearly cried. The top was in shreds; one side of the car was missing, and the doors were lying on what was left of the back seat. It was a disaster! But Senior's first prize came early on when it received a trophy from the Michigan Region of the Classic Car Club of America for, The Biggest Challenge of the Year Award!! Shelly, undaunted by the award, eagerly accepted the mantle.

Stern's Mercedes exhibited for six months at
the 100th anniversary of Mercedes Benz exhibit,
Behring Museum, Walnut Creek, California

After $200,000, much heartache, many hours and years of hard work, and lots of fun, we finally decided it was time for Senior to find a new home. Senior took many honorable awards, including plaques from the Meadowbrook Concourse of Cars, Pebble Beach

Concourse d'Elegance and, ironically, First Place for a Perfect Restoration from the same Classic Car Club of America, Michigan Region, which had so insulted him at the outset of Shelly's project. Senior also resided for six months in the famous Blackhawk Old Car Museum in Walnut Creek, California as part of an exhibit honoring the "100th Anniversary of Mercedes Benz". When we sold Senior for $125,000, we were heartsick at the failure of our investment. The old car market had just taken a huge nose dive, but in spite of our huge financial loss, Senior had given us a great ride!

The 1980s were a notable time for us. From the time we moved to Michigan, our family fell in love with the northern part of Michigan's Lower Peninsula, which Michiganders refer to as, "up north". Beginning with one-week summer vacations in a cottage on the beach at Traverse City when the kids were young, this love affair intensified over the years.

In the late 1970s we started thinking about getting a place of our own. By then, Gayle and Jeremy had graduated high school, and were busy with their own lives. But Shelly and I had not outgrown our passion and need for the North Country. We started looking around in earnest. We weren't sure we could afford this venture but decided looking didn't cost anything.

We were familiar with the Traverse City area, having upgraded from our cottage days on Grand Traverse Bay to the Homestead, a lovely condo resort northwest of Traverse City, where we vacationed with the kids for a week every summer for several years. We thought seriously about buying a condo there, until Jeremy suggested that the Petoskey/Harbor Springs area was not as isolated, yet equally beautiful and easier to get to from Franklin. He thought we would be happier there. We remembered being impressed by the area on earlier visits there, so we decided to investigate.

Harbor Springs, Michigan – one of our favorite spots

Jeremy was right. There was more to do there, and we found a bigger selection of places to rent and purchase. Our friends, Ruth and Julian Lefkowitz were interested in a place, too. We thought a partnership with them made sense. We came up regularly together to look.

One evening Shelly and I walked into a popular restaurant in Harbor Springs for dinner. Sitting at the first table were Steve Victor, a good friend of Anita and Ralph Sosin. He was sitting with Norman Jaslov, Steve's friend who was president of the little Temple in Petoskey, and a member of Birchwood Farms Country Club where we had played golf a few times. We told them we were looking around with friends for a place to buy. Norman slapped the table, saying, with great conviction, "I have the perfect place for you". Norman, it turned out, was a partner in a new development between Petoskey and Harbor Springs called the Lakeside Club. We made a date to get a tour of the place.

It was a fall day I shall never forget. The weather was "up-north perfect." We entered Number 10, a brand new, architecturally modern two-bedroom, three-bath unit with a loft. I was immediately smitten by its huge windows, sliding glass doors and high ceilings. The light actually poured in, bringing the mesmerizing outdoor surroundings with it. Even the loft and the master bedroom overlooked the lake.

When we walked out on the deck, I reached out and touched a large white birch tree. At that moment my heart started to pound, and my knees got weak. The sky was a blanket of blue, a nip of autumn was in the air and 10 yards in front of me was Round Lake, the sweetest little lake I had ever seen. Shelly and I looked at each other, and we both knew -- This was it!

The Lefkowitzes and the Sterns had already decided that each family needed its own place. A number of months after we bought "The Perfect 10," the unit adjoining ours went on the market, and the Lefkowitzes became our neighbors. We called our place "Paradise," they called their place, "The Cottage Next to Paradise."

It was a life enhancing experience for both our families for 23 years. In 2005, we decided to sell our up-north condo; it felt like the right thing to do to both of us, but our memories will last forever.

Sunrise on Little Round Lake, Petoskey, Michigan, viewed from our condominium

Round Lake from "Paradise"

The car nuts from Detroit in their 1975 Oldsmobile convertible - at the Harbor Springs, Michigan 4rth of July parade

One evening in the mid 1990s, I was doing the dishes and Shelly was in the den. He was watching Wagner's "Ring Cycle" on PBS. Suddenly, he called to me, "Jess, Jess, come in here, you won't believe it!" I responded firmly. "Shelly, you know I hate Wagner. The music is awful, and he was a vicious anti-Semite. I'm not interested." Silence. Five minutes later, "Jess, you have got to hear this. It is amazing." My turn -- "Shelly, I told you I hate Wagner." Again, "Jess, p-l-e-a-s-e come in for just a minute. The story is sensational, and the music is beautiful."

By then I was finished with the dishes. I couldn't stand more of Shelly's pleading, it was so intense. "Alright, I'll come in for a couple of minutes to appease you, but don't expect me to stay." Shelly gave me a brief synopsis. I sat down prepared to remain for maybe five minutes. Ten minutes later I was caught up in the power of the story, and, to my utter amazement, I was touched by the gorgeous sound emanating from our TV.

The "Ring Cycle" consists of four operas, rarely produced as single operas. The combined experience requires 15 hours. The individual live operas are usually scheduled during a one-week period with one or two day breaks between each opera. We watched the PBS series for four straight nights. We were irrevocably hooked.

When the TV production ended, without any hesitation we both decided we wanted to experience the Ring Cycle live as soon as possible. It is an extremely expensive enterprise and is not done in the United States that often in very many venues.

More than a year went by. One day Shelly showed me a small ad in the Metropolitan Opera's newsletter announcing a forthcoming production of the Ring Cycle in June, 1998 by the Arizona Opera in Flagstaff. Comparatively speaking, the operas were reasonably priced. I remembered that Flagstaff was not far from Sedona, a city famous for its red rocks, and only a few hours from the Grand Canyon, as well. Since the operas were scheduled for every other day, Shelly agreed to my suggestion that we do it all. I immediately went to work, ordering the opera tickets, reserving two nights before the operas started at Enchantment, the famous resort hotel in Sedona. Within a few hours, the deed was done, and we were both very excited.

We bought tapes of the complete performance of the Ring Cycle, listening to every note, studying the myriad motifs Wagner used to represent character, events and moods. We seriously studied the homework necessary to properly prepare for our forthcoming experience.

About three weeks before we were to depart for Arizona I was diagnosed with breast cancer and scheduled for immediate surgery. The thought of canceling our trip added to my anguish. I decided to discuss this dilemma with both my oncologist and my surgeon. They both agreed, the surgery was not an emergency and urged me to take the trip. Shelly and I dwelled on this option for days until I reached a point of relief and comfort with the decision to go ahead with our longed for trip. I just knew it was the right thing to do. I rescheduled the surgery for June 16, Monday at 7 a.m., the day after we were to return from Arizona.

For both of us, the Ring Cycle was the greatest artistic experience of our lives. Shelly and I held hands during the four operas. Not knowing what the future held for us made every moment and every note more precious. And our stop in Sedona, known for being a healing place, offered a spiritual atmosphere which helped prepare me for my treatment.

In spite of our love for Wagner's music, there remained a disturbing paradox with which we had to come to terms. Wagner's anti-Semitism continued to be a huge problem for us. How could anyone who wrote a story about redemptive love, and composed its gorgeous music be such a hateful person? We spent hours at the University of Arizona library in Flagstaff reading books on the subject of Wagner's problem with the Jews. Our studies did not offer an absolute answer to our dilemma.

We finally realized the answer did not reside in scholarly treatises. Instead, the issue needed to be addressed on a personal level by Shelly and me. We both came to the conclusion that human behavior portrayed in art is not always compatible with the artist's nature and character. Wagner was a despicable human being, but a great artist. When we watch his operas and listen to his music, we are transported to the realm of high art. We will always be troubled by the dilemma but are managing to live with it.

BLESSINGS
Berachot

As I reflect on my life, I believe that writing this memoir has, on a profound level, been a story of discovery -- a search for my true self. These ponderings have led me to conclude that I have had more than my share of blessings.

As defined by Webster, a blessing is, "A thing conducive to happiness." Experience has taught me that it was only when I internalized an event, acknowledging it as something special, that the moment was transformed and became a blessing. Blessings are best understood when they are labeled as such by the recipient. Many of my blessings started out as challenges, which with the help of insight, determination and persistence, were transformed into blessings.

This process was enabled when I discovered I could identify my challenging issues by immersing myself, as in a deep and cloudy pond, over and over again, asking these questions with each immersion. Am I growing as a person? (This in my case does not mean am I getting taller). Am I becoming kinder and more compassionate to myself and to others? Am I willing to confront my fears and do battle with them? Do I realize how fortunate I am? By these standards, my immersions have yielded starting points for identifying my challenges/blessings!

I grew up scared. Don't ask me why, I just did. Terror and fear surrounded me. As a child I was afraid of loud noises. Parades and steam ship whistles started me screaming. I was terrified of getting my teeth brushed even though the dentist was my uncle. As I became an adult, those childhood fears were replaced by others: fear of flying and, most markedly, an overwhelmingly severe panic fear of skiing and chair lifts.

I was about 50 years old when I got a phone call from my brother. "Jess, when are you and Shelly coming out to Denver to visit and go skiing with us?" "Irving, you have to be kidding," I said. "I am terrified of skiing."

There was a pause, indicating his incredulousness. "Jess, you know I love sports and I have to tell you, skiing is the most fun sport experience I have ever had. You don't know what you're missing." Despite my fear, I had to admit to myself that skiing had an alluring mystique about it. The clothes, the youth and vigor of the sport, the entire appeal of such glamorous settings as the Alps, the Rocky Mountains and, even Northern Michigan gave skiing an unattainable allure. I had friends who loved it. And now my brother confirmed the magic of the sport. What was I to do? I was trapped by my fear.

Within moments of my conversation with Irving, I was overtaken by a powerful urge. I became possessed. My heart rate tripled, my brain became a fantasyland. As I began pounding my desk and swearing at myself, I noticed my hand was simultaneously reaching for the telephone. In those few seconds I was propelled by an inexplicable and sudden force. Without hesitating, I picked up the phone, set a date with my brother and made airlines reservations for Denver. When I announced this momentous decision to Shelly, he was flabbergasted and delighted.

The next day with the benefit of a payload of adrenaline, I bought skis and boots and a great looking ski outfit. I also selected the necessary garments and equipment for Shelly and advised him to get over to the Sport House to try them on. I still thought I might wake up the next day to find my transformation had been a dream and that the real Jessie had returned to haunt me again, but she did not return.

A few months later, we were on a flight to Denver. While I realized I had not gotten over my fear of skiing, a determination to win the battle and become "normal" had been deeply ensconced in my heart and brain. I never wavered for a minute about the trip out west. From Denver, we drove with Irving and Carol to Steam Boat Springs, a lovely ski area where Irving had made reservations. I cannot remember anything about the hotel, but I shall never forget what followed our arrival there.

The first day Shelly and I signed up for lessons. New skiers were required to take a short chair lift ride to a testing area. For me it was a very long ride. I held Shelly's hand and talked to myself on the ride up, reminding myself over and over that my fear was irrational, that I had to get over it and start having fun.

I barely survived that first chair lift experience. When I got to the edge of the testing hill and looked down the hill, I nearly fainted as tears began flowing.

I was painfully embarrassed. A good looking male ski instructor comforted me. "It's okay. Don't worry. I'll get you back down to the base. Just put your head on my back, your arms around me and your skis between mine. You'll be down in no time, maybe one minute." I felt safe and actually relaxed on the way down. He was also very cute. My savior deposited me on the bunny hill with the three to eight year olds. Soon I got the hang of snow-plowing and could actually make some nice turns. By the end of the day, I was ready to tackle the mountain again.

The biggest hurdle was my fear of the chair lift, a fear so out of control that every time I got on the chair I felt an urge to jump off. I had a dry mouth, sweaty palms, racing heart, dilated pupils and an awful feeling in my gut. It was obvious that this was not going to be easy. I had a demon at work that did not want to give up its power to control me and was determined to keep me from having a good time. But the demon had a problem, too. I was ready for a fight. A huge battle raged between that demon and my determination to neutralize and destroy my foe. I kept telling myself that if I just got strong enough and mad enough, I would succeed. The outcome was in the hands of the mighty -- strength and will would win the contest.

The matter was still not settled on the second day. Shelly had to hold my hand once again going up the mountain, and I still had all the physical symptoms of the previous morning. I tried to mobilize the forces of positive thinking, saying out loud -- very loudly -- with frequency and conviction, "Look at all the people on the chair lift talking and having fun. They're laughing, swinging their feet, enjoying the gorgeous scenery and having a great time. You are the only jerk, Jessie. You do not need this ridiculous fear anymore. I am furious at this nonsense. Knock it off. Want to start relaxing and having fun? You can do it. Feel the positive energy you have inside yourself. YOU CAN DO IT." And so the battle raged.

On the third day, I was able to look down the mountain as I cautiously and very slowly began my decent making huge traverses. It was not a dream! When I finally got to the bottom of the run, however, my friend the chair lift was still silently awaiting me. I reluctantly boarded, and my monologue would begin again and again, getting fiercer and more determined with each repetition.

After a few more runs, I noticed I was more relaxed and my traverses were less extreme and, remarkably, less dreaded. Even the chair lift rides were punctuated by moments of normal conversation with Shelly and brief moments of diminished terror. A few lift rides later came one of the profoundest moments of my life. I got on the chair prepared for the usual ugly feeling in my gut, but it was gone! My eyes filled with tears, followed by a scream of triumph which could have been heard in Detroit. At that moment I learned the true meaning of the word ecstasy!

By the end of the week I was appreciating the gorgeous surroundings, skiing the green (easiest) runs and successfully starting to make parallel turns. Remarkably, the effect of my ski adventure was a "package deal." On the return flight to Detroit I was overjoyed to discover my fear of flying had evaporated, too.

I had won a battle. It is not necessary to hold on to parts of yourself that are harmful. Change is possible! I was filled with wonder and gratitude. Since then, skiing has added a dimension to my life and to that of our family. Shelly loves to ski, as do Gayle and Jeremy. The icing on the cake is that our six grandchildren all partake of this exciting and fun activity. If that isn't a blessing, what is?

In Colorado with our favorite winter sport

About 10 days after our terrible roll over accident in Junior, my neck started hurting. I had heard of whip lash injuries but thought I had escaped that fate. However, escape was not in the cards. I had no idea pain could be so persistent. I tried everything: pain medication, hot and cold applications, physical therapy, wearing a collar, prayer and tears. Nothing worked. I had x-rays and other tests that indicated I had arthritis as well as a slipped disc in my neck. I took this diagnosis seriously, and felt very sorry for myself.

About a year into my agony we were invited to friends for dinner when the subject turned to back trouble. We listened to each other's horror stories, each person impatiently awaiting their turn, certain that their tale would be the most horrific. The conversation took a turn when our host said to his guests, "I have a book to suggest: Healing Back Pain, by Dr John Sarno. Try it." The next day I rushed to the book store and made my purchase.

Dr. Sarno, director of the Department of Physical Medicine at Columbia University had made a remarkable discovery. He noted that the incidence of back and neck problems had reached epidemic proportions. At the same time he noticed that some patients with disc and other back and neck disorders never complained of pain while other patients with the exact same x-ray and MRI results experienced severe pain. This made no sense to Sarno, so he decided to get to the bottom of this bewildering phenomenon.

After years of patient interviews and study, he concluded that a reduction of blood to the painful area was causing the involved muscles to go into spasm. He found no physiological explanation for the blood flow to be impaired, nor were there any clinical implications to explain the reason why two patients with the exact same MRIs, X-rays and medical histories should differ so drastically in suffering. In some of his patients, the pain was psychologically induced. In other words, it was a mind/body problem, with no medical or clinical basis.

This position intrigued me, and I decided to accept Dr. Sarno's theory and follow the radical regime he suggested, which included accepting that there were many people with the same medical ailments I had who had no pain, and to accept the fact that I could be in charge of this matter. Success required giving up the collar, the pain medication and the incessant exercises and 15-minute hot showers. After 10 days of constant attentiveness to the challenge at hand, which took relentless hard work, I woke up one day completely free of pain. I was miraculously cured. I am still in awe of this transformation.

But I still needed to understand what happened to my brain after the accident, which precipitated the problem.

The answer was found when I reviewed my reaction to the details of the accident. I was driving Junior, when I noticed the front door on the driver's side was ajar. Junior had suicide doors, which opened from the front, with the hinges behind the driver. When I instinctively opened the door (less than an inch) to slam it shut, we were going about 60 miles an hour on the expressway. The door flew open causing the car to go wildly out of control. In a matter of seconds, we swerved into the left lane, back into the right lane and finally down a steep embankment into a ditch. Junior rolled over.

Luckily, we were not thrown out of the car on the expressway. Junior had no seat belts. After a thorough examination in the emergency room, they discharged us because we had no fractures, which was a mistake. We were both in pain and could not walk. Our wonderful neighbors, Ralph and Miles came to pick us up. When we got home, we were in deplorable shape. We needed nursing. Our angels of mercy, Anita and Evie were waiting for us at home. Anita managed to get me in the bathtub to clean me up. My hair was filthy, and my face was black and blue and swollen beyond recognition. Shelly could not manage the stairs, so we slept on our pull-out couch in the den. Evie, stayed over all night to care for us. We both decided how lucky we were to have the Sosins and the Zemans as neighbors.

Several years later after reading Dr. Sarno, I realized that the automobile accident had likely induced a huge dose of remorse and guilt. After all, I was the driver and caused the accident by opening the car door. It became obvious to me that my conscience could simply not deal with these facts. As soon as I accepted Dr. Sarno's theory and began following his suggestions, my neck pain subsided and my admiration for this brilliant doctor has never wavered. Nor has my neck pain returned. This experience has made me acutely sensitive to the power of the mind/body connection and its impact on my life.

This autobiography would not be complete without paying tribute to our children. They have been our greatest blessing. Both Gayle and Jeremy are wonderful human beings. Bright, resilient, honorable, fun and humane, they have strong constitutions and lots of character. We adore them and are very proud of them, their spouses and their children.

Gayle steadfastly followed her dream of becoming a dancer. I'll never forget the day she left for the University of Wisconsin. She chose that school because it was the first major university to institute a Modern Dance major. When I took her to the airport to leave for Madison on her new adventure I knew she was excited. I was very happy for her, but I never expected what happened next. We hugged and said goodbye, and I wished her good luck. As I watched her walk away, I crumbled, fighting back tears. It finally hit me that this moment was the beginning of her own adventure. She would never be my little girl again.

Gayle, the dancer

Nothing has given Shelly and me more pleasure over the years than watching Gayle perform when she was with the Harbinger Dance Company. Although, she is no longer a professional dancer, my need to see her dance remains. I desperately need a fix once in a while. Fortunately, she takes a couple of ballet classes a week. And her teacher has an annual open class which Shelly and I never miss. We still melt when we see her dance. She is also a marvelous mother, Pilates instructor, ballet teacher and friend. Everyone loves and admires her and, besides, she makes a wicked apple pie, fabulous chicken soup and matzah balls which are the envy of every Jewish cook!!

As for Jeremy -- besides a delightful personality, his hallmark has been his strength of character best exemplified by his many friendships from childhood on. I remember the day Tom, Jeremy and a few other friends were scheduled to go up north for the weekend. That morning, Tom came over on his new bike, which he parked at the bottom of our driveway. He met with Jeremy to talk about their plans for departure. When he left about thirty minutes later, the bike had been stolen. Tom called his dad who arrived at our house minutes later in a rage about the bike. He was so furious he would not let Tom go up north. To further punish him, he said he had to work off the cost of the new bike beginning "today." Though the other boys were still planning to leave, Jeremy elected to forfeit the trip and, instead worked the rest of the day with Tom in a 90 degree heat wave, pulling out the biggest weeds I had ever seen to help his friend begin paying his dad for the bike. Jeremy also turned over the money he earned that dreadful day to Tom.

Emily, Gary, Gayle, and Noah

Academically, Jeremy was a late bloomer. He started making good grades in eleventh grade when he transferred to Cranbrook, a first-rate private school in our area. That move, and Jeremy's hard work, managed to get him an acceptance at the University of Michigan. After graduation, he worked for a year or so before deciding to go to law school. He finished number one in his class his freshman year at University of Detroit Law School. He insisted on going to night school for his law degree, so he could continue working during the day and not be a financial burden on his parents. His character shone again. He has distinguished himself as a respected and brilliant communications lawyer and is well known in his field. He plays guitar with gusto and has a great future as a photographer. He is the devoted father of Joshua, Ari, Eban and Seth who bring him his greatest pleasure.

Front Row: Eban and Seth, Back row:
Jeremy, Josh, Hildy, and Ari

We are fortunate. Both of our children are bright resilient, honorable, fun and humane. We adore them and are proud of them and their spouses. I want to pay special tribute to Gary and Hildy, our amazing in-law children and thank them for teaching me so much.

A word about our grandchildren. Emily, our eldest grandchild, has the distinction-which she savors-of being our only girl. She has always been a joy. She is bright, beautiful and determined. While she was achieving an undergraduate degree in science at Michigan State

University, she decided she wanted to pursue a graduate degree in medicine. She is now applying to several medical schools. She has all the qualities necessary to becoming a wonderful doctor. Her grandfather is especially thrilled with her decision, and we wish her well.

Her brother, Noah is currently a senior at West Bloomfield High School, and applying to several universities and colleges. He is our tallest Stern, so far. He has happily received a proper dose of genes from Gary, his dad and is not only tall and handsome, but delights us with his engaging personality, a wonderful trait, which if he applies himself in college, should lead him down a path of success.

In Manhattan Beach, California we are blessed with four grandsons. Joshua, the eldest is now 15 years old. He is bright, serious, kind and quietly loving with blond hair and beautiful brown eyes. He is reputed to look like me, his proud Granny.

Ari, at thirteen, gave his grandparents a thrill in the summer of 2007, when he celebrated his Bar Mitzvah. Ari is outgoing, and an amazing scholar and student. Furthermore, he is not wanting in physical attributes. His brown hair and blue eyes serve him in good stead. He is also thoughtful, considerate and fun as well as a budding poet and writer.

Nine-year-old Eban is exuberant, talented and loving. He gets good grades in school, plays three musical instruments, loves to laugh and has huge amounts of energy, some of which is directed to his love of sports. His black hair, brown eyes and huge smile will win friends and influence people on any path he chooses.

Hildy's and Jeremy's youngest is also irresistible. Seth has brown hair which matches his bronze complexion, making his huge dark brown eyes sparkle and dance. He is very perceptive, and it is a joy to discuss any and all subjects with him. His wit and love of laughter are expressions of his essence.

Both our Detroit and Los Angeles kids love and participate in team sports, as well as in skiing. Whether in sports or in academics, it seems everything they do, they do well.

And here I enter the realm of my biggest surprise blessing of all. Ironically, breast cancer has brought me many gifts. It was a beautiful spring day in late May, 1998, when Shelly casually announced he had an errand to run. Instead of waiting until the next day for my surgeon to call with the biopsy report, Shelly, not surprisingly, decided to take matters into his own hands. Without telling me where he was going, he went to the laboratory to get the results directly from the pathologist. I was restlessly trying to relax on the couch in our living room when he returned less than an hour later. As soon as I saw his drawn face, I knew. When he reported that the tumor was positive, a huge wave of relief engulfed me as I blurted out, "Now I don't have to be scared anymore."

I could not believe I had said that. But I knew what I said was true and that having said it made everything different. From that moment on I was able to accept the reality of my cancer, even the dreaded treatment. My terror was gone. I did not think about it then, but I realize now what a transitional moment that was. Amazingly, I felt at peace and was very much aware that something miraculous had just occurred. I believe it was a blessing.

As a result of my diagnosis, extraordinary people have come into my life that have given me strength, taught me much and enriched my life. The rest is history, beginning with the following story.

I was meeting with my oncologist for the first time when he suggested that I might want to take advantage of the service of the oncology social worker, Linda Diaz, who worked for Sinai Hospital. I decided it would be a good idea to avail myself of all the help I could get. Within our first few sessions I told Linda my life story. We laughed, I cried, and she told me about Mindfulness Meditation.

Struck by her warmth, her ability to really listen and by her wisdom, Linda taught me that nothing of consequence that happens in one's life is a coincidence. The more I reflect on my life the more I am convinced how true that is. When she felt I no longer needed her as a therapist, we became friends. Linda, thank you for coming into my life, for sharing your family with me, for introducing me to Mindfulness Meditation as well as suggesting wonderful books which have helped me advance my quest for personal growth. We have a lot of history. And yes, the fun. Let's not forget the fun.

Joan Mann had been a sorority sister at Indiana University. I liked her from the start, but we never became close friends until after we moved to Michigan, when we rediscovered each other one night at Howard Johnson's, a popular late night refreshment hangout. We recognized each other and decided to make a date. From time to time over the next 20 years, we would go out together with our husbands.

In 1998 when she heard I had been diagnosed with breast cancer, she called to commiserate. When I told her I was going to start my chemotherapy, she promptly shocked me by saying, "I will take you to all of your treatments and keep you company." I was touched by her amazing offer but demurred, assuring her it was a five-minute drive, and I was relaxed about getting my treatments. "Besides," I said, "Shelly will probably go with me the first time." But Joan had made up her mind! She started showing up for my treatments. She was terrific company, and believe it or not, we had lots of laughs. It made the two to four hours fly. I have continued to be awed by her demonstration of friendship and caring. I consider Joan Mann one of my serious blessings.

And there have been many others. Howard Schubiner, whom I met through Linda, has become a cherished friend and my meditation guru. The women who are in my breast cancer support group have become very dear to me. We have come to know each other well as we share our lives with one another on a profound level.

Amal, my hypnotist knows me better than anyone else and has helped me get to know myself. Amal and hypnosis are, gratefully, my blessings.

There are other blessings which cancer has brought me. Both yoga and mindfulness meditation which came into my life after my diagnosis have shown me that the magic of the breath opens the heart, allowing and encouraging the possibility of change.

Now that I have acknowledged those challenges and issues which morphed into blessings, I can turn to other treasured blessings. These came to me without baggage. No challenges or caveats. Instead they were obvious, simple but vital blessings of my life. I will begin with my family.

And, finally, my greatest blessing, and challenge, has been 55 years of marriage to Shelly Stern, the love of my life. As much as I love to write, I could never find the words to describe how much I cherish him, admire him and depend on him. He has never let me down. I will rely on Shelly's beautiful and often stated quote to sum up our relationship, "Ours is a marriage made in heaven."

Detroit Federation Israel Mission Bus Captains, 2004

Speaking about this memoir, of late, Shelly too frequently asks, "Aren't you finished yet?" I think he wants this project finished, so I can go to more movies with him.

And let it be said. Shelly is the most resourceful person I have ever met. I have often told people that if I were stranded on an uninhabited island with Shelly, I would not have a single worry! He would know exactly what to do and how to do it. He never gives up when challenged. Instead, he always has a new idea. And, incidentally, he can fix and make anything from scratch. I have no doubt that if we wanted to leave the island, Shelly would get us home.

In addition to family, I have been extraordinarily blessed with friends, old and new, whom I truly love. These amazing people honor me with their friendship. I say to each of them. I look forward to many more years of joyful relationship. You have no idea how much I need you.

Here is an example of such a friendship. As I went through the cafeteria line one evening my first year at the University of Michigan's Bear River Writers' Conference, I noticed that the roast offering looked too light to be lamb or beef. I inquired what it was. "It's a pork roast," said the nice lady behind the counter. I thanked her and said, "I don't eat pork. I'll have the fish." A voice behind me said, "Oh, are you Jewish?" I looked up discovering a tall, attractive woman with an engaging smile. "Yes," I said. Her smile broadened. "So am I—almost. I am in the process of converting."

I felt an immediate connection with her. We had dinner together. Her name is Pia Taavila. She is a gifted published poet and teaches English at Gallaudet University, a college for the deaf in Washington, D.C. By the time the conference ended we knew each other well. She read several of her poems to me and she was the first person with whom I had dared to share one of my poems that first year at Bear River. Becoming a Jew was the current centerpiece of her life. I acknowledged how much my Jewish heritage meant to me. We talked about everything from Judaism to writing, to the problems of the world. And through it all, we had fun.

We continued to communicate via the internet. When I saw her next in 2006, her conversion was complete. We celebrated with hugs and more precious togetherness. We were taking a walk, doing more "Jewish talking," when Pia said, "I get great comfort knowing one day I will be buried in my tallit." It was an amazing comment, something I had never thought about. I replied, "I don't own a tallit. Shelly has one but I don't." "It would give me great pleasure to give you one," she said. "I have two." For a moment I was speechless. "Pia, I can't let you do that. Tallitot are very expensive." I said. "I am so moved by the offer but…"

Without hesitating, my friend continued to insist that it would mean a great deal to her to give me the tallit. She said I had been an inspiration to her when we first met, that it was fitting that I have the tallit. I received it in the mail a few weeks later. It is the most beautiful tallit I have ever seen. When I put it on for the first time at services in Petoskey that summer, I felt safe and more connected to my heritage than ever. I love my tallit and will forever think of Pia every time I wear it. A friend like that is indeed a blessing.

I believe I am happiest when I am engaged with people. I have found such a group of people at Karma-Yoga, a very special and loving place where I have made many friends. Karma-Yoga specializes in great hugs! Yoga, meditation, my family and my Jewish heritage are not only blessings. They are the anchors of my life. They sustain me, helping to keep me from wallowing in self pity, self-righteousness and victimization. I have learned that I can change the way I react. One's conditioned responses can be reconditioned! I am more centered in the peacefulness of "being" and less in the busyness of "doing."

For the first time in my life, I enjoy spending time alone. I am more comfortable in my own skin, more aware of the essential part of who I am and more tolerant of others. Most of my days are filled with love and a sense of wholeness and joy. My story is not unique. At its center are the universal yearnings and challenges all humans encounter. We all find reflections of ourselves in sacred myths, in literature and in our human relationships. The wonder of it is that healing, personal growth and love are available to everyone.

The great challenge of our global family today can best be presented as a question. Why does this body part we call the heart which pumps blood to the rest of the body, including the brain, remain our fractured world's last best hope?

I think one of the reasons it has taken me so long to complete this memoir is the very nature of the task suggests that once the project is complete, it is as if one's life is over -- that there will be no more stories to tell, no more sentences to write, that the final period will, indeed, be the last. Nonsense. Every moment offers a new beginning. I eagerly await the epilogue.

Life offers each of us chances that begins with our first breath and the first beat of our heart and ends we know not when. What is open-ended for us humans is the limitless possibility of living mindfully, with each breath and each heartbeat. I am reminded of the story of the man walking down Fifth Avenue carrying a violin who stops a bystander to ask, "Excuse me, sir, how do I get to Carnegie Hall?" The gentleman replies," Practice, practice, practice."

As I contemplate my 78th birthday, gratitude, approbation and love bring me to a place of tremendous affirmation of life and a matchless sense of peace. I feel prepared for what awaits me, including the inevitable end of the journey. Writing this memoir has prepared me for that too. Not that it is possible to ever reach a perfect conclusion. It is not the moment we reach that elusive destination that matters. Rather it is the path we walk moment by moment.

My goal for the rest of my life is to practice reminding myself to never miss a beat.

EPILOGUE

I must take notes

I must take notes
My heart speaks
I must take notes
So I have been instructed
By a wise friend
Listen to its beat
The power the joy
The possibilities for healing
Flowing from an open heart
Lessons from childhood often neglected
Leaving the heart aching
Its mechanical beat
Only a shadow of its potential
It seems a waste
Yet so human
To accept such a crippling matter

Blocking the heart's true destiny
To open fully alive
To chorus its rhythms
With other singing hearts
To hear the whole world sing
Human beings connecting
An anthem of life
Honoring each other
And the gift of the heart